Organizing Successful Tournaments

THIRD EDITION

John Byl, PhD

Redeemer University College
Ancaster, Ontario

HUMAN KINETICS

Library of Congress Cataloging-in-Publication Data

Byl, John.
  Organizing successful tournaments / John Byl.-- 3rd ed.
    p. cm.
  ISBN 0-7360-5952-0 (soft cover)
  1. Sports administration. 2. Sports tournaments--Management. I. Title.
  GV713.B95 2005
  796'.069   2005027058

ISBN-10: 0-7360-5952-0
ISBN-13: 978-0-7360-5952-7

Acquisitions Editor: Jana Hunter
Managing Editor: Wendy McLaughlin
Assistant Editor: Kim Thoren
Copyeditor: John Wentworth
Proofreader: Erin Cler
Graphic Designer: Nancy Rasmus
Graphic Artist: Kim McFarland
Photo Manager: Dan Wendt
Cover Designer: Keith Blomberg
Photographer (cover): © Human Kinetics
Art Manager: Kareema McLendon-Foster
Illustrator: Kim McFarland
Printer: United Graphics

Human Kinetics books are available at special discounts for bulk purchase. Special editions or book excerpts can also be created to specification. For details, contact the Special Sales Manager at Human Kinetics.

Printed in the United States of America   10 9 8 7 6 5 4 3 2 1

Human Kinetics
Web site: www.HumanKinetics.com

United States: Human Kinetics
P.O. Box 5076
Champaign, IL 61825-5076
800-747-4457
e-mail: humank@hkusa.com

Canada: Human Kinetics
475 Devonshire Road Unit 100
Windsor, ON N8Y 2L5
800-465-7301 (in Canada only)
e-mail: orders@hkcanada.com

Europe: Human Kinetics
107 Bradford Road
Stanningley
Leeds LS28 6AT, United Kingdom
+44 (0) 113 255 5665
e-mail: hk@hkeurope.com

Australia: Human Kinetics
57A Price Avenue
Lower Mitcham, South Australia 5062
08 8277 1555
e-mail: liaw@hkaustralia.com

New Zealand: Human Kinetics
Division of Sports Distributors NZ Ltd.
P.O. Box 300 226 Albany
North Shore City
Auckland
0064 9 448 1207
e-mail: info@humankinetics.co.nz

To Mom and Dad.

Thanks for your love and support.

CONTENTS

PREFACE

This book and accompanying CD will make the scheduling of even the most complicated tournaments and leagues a very efficient process. The text explains the scheduling process and offers photocopy-ready forms to use. The CD contains more than 1,000 ready-to-use schedules that take little time to complete; the forms can be readily printed or saved to your Web page. As the event host, you will be organized and efficient, and, most important, you will be able to provide the participants with a great schedule.

Whether you are a physical educator, a coach, a director of athletics, in charge of intramurals, or involved in organizing a community league, you often use tournaments and leagues to help organize people at play. Without a doubt you have experienced some of the frustrations associated with organizing and participating in tournaments and leagues, such as finding that a player or team has dropped out at the last minute; finding an error in the schedule halfway through a league, which resulted in great confusion; one or two teams playing most of their games on the worst court or field; and becoming discouraged about a tournament format because it eliminated poor players too quickly or because the tournament took too long or had too many games. And you might have avoided using an organized system because the preparation was too time consuming.

This manual and CD are designed to alleviate some of these problems and to assist you in several ways. The most commonly used tournaments are presented in this book: single and double elimination, multilevel, four different round robins, and several extended tournaments such as the ladder or pyramid.

Chapter 1 explains the major strengths and weaknesses of each type of schedule. This will help you select the type that best suits your goals. Once you have selected the most appropriate type, you simply need to turn to the chapter and schedule on the CD devoted to your preferred tournament or league, where you will find your work made considerably easier. Chapters 2-7 begin with an explanation of relevant details involved in implementing a particular tournament. A seeding chart is also provided to ensure the best possible quality of play. Finally, the actual draw sheets and the playing schedules for the relevant number of playing areas are included. Once you have selected a scheduling type, a ranking of the participants should be completed; participants' names are then placed on the draw sheet according to the seeding table, and the schedule is ready and play can begin. Your problem-free tournament and league are prepared simply and quickly.

Chapter 8 explains the process of assigning seeds and understanding byes. Tiebreaking procedures for a variety of sports and tournaments are provided in chapter 9, and chapter 10 will give you some hints on how to plan and conduct a worry-free tournament.

I wish you well in your exciting role as tournament director.

ACKNOWLEDGMENTS

This book was made possible through the assistance of several institutions and people. I first wish to thank Redeemer University College and its support community for making it possible for me to work on this book. In particular, I would like to thank Jeannette Grasman, Christine Mantel, Matt Byl, and Aleida VanderWoerd, who helped with a lot of the more tedious computer entries and calculations.

The CD is a major breakthrough in providing great schedules that can be quickly and easily produced. Frank Byl, from www.powerconcepts.ca, was most helpful in teaching me some of the applications that make these schedules so powerful and easy.

I am also very appreciative of the work that Human Kinetics is doing and the kind of support they are providing for those involved in physical education and sport. Their careful assistance in the production of this book is also appreciated. In particular I want to thank Jana Hunter and Wendy McLaughlin for their supportive assistance.

The chapter on extended tournaments is borrowed from Boyden and Burton's book *Staging Successful Tournaments*. Permission to use their work is appreciated.

I owe a lot of thanks to the following people who double-checked the thousands of pages of schedules: Christine Mantel, Julianne Bosman, Carrie Heidbuurt, Dawn Johnson, Winona Siebenga, and Marieka Van Walderveen.

I wish to thank my wife, Catherine, who, in the preparation of this book and always, has given so much to me in so many different ways. Thanks for your love.

CHAPTER 1

Types and Selection of Tournaments and Leagues

Whether you are hosting a national basketball tournament, organizing a city soccer league, putting together a horseshoe tournament at a camp, or holding a chess tournament in your home, this book makes scheduling your event very easy. Tournament and league hosts might decide to choose a tournament or league type they are most familiar with and go directly to the chapter dealing with that type. However, this choice of tournament may or may not be the best one. This chapter outlines the strengths and limitations of each tournament and league type and explains the more detailed principles in determining seeding, byes, and assignment of game numbers and locations.

As a tournament or league director, you might have various reasons for how you choose to organize participants in a tournament or league. Most often, the primary goal in using leagues and tournaments is to determine the ranking of participants or to provide a structure within which ranking is possible. You will also undoubtedly have subgoals, which will be affected by the availability of time and facilities. In developing your subgoals, you must clearly answer questions such as these:

- Do I want all players to play an equal number of games?
- Does it matter if the number of games is the same per player?
- Do I want all the games to be closely contested?
- Does it matter if there are a few lopsided games?
- How important is it to know who comes in first, second, third, fourth, or fifth?

How you answer these questions will help you decide which type of tournament or league to use.

Time and facilities will sometimes limit your options, and you might need to compromise in some areas. You must make a realistic assessment of the number of games required for various tournament and league types and of the time it takes to complete a schedule considering the number of locations available. However, first you should establish goals for your tournament and league, and then determine how realistic these goals are in terms of time and facilities. If you need to compromise, keep close to your goals. Helpful evaluations of each tournament and league type follow; table 1.1 on page 6 summarizes this information.

Once you complete this decision-making process, the remaining work is straightforward. You can use the schedules in this book or the ones on the CD. The book explains the construction and benefits of various tournament and league types and provides selected draw sheets that can be photocopied. The CD provides over 1,000 great schedules that can be easily and quickly produced, providing a clean printed copy. To operate the program on the CD, you must have Microsoft Word. The program works equally well on a PC or a Mac.

To use the book, turn to the appropriate chapter, find the draw sheet for the required number of entries, and photocopy it. Seed entries and place their names on the draw sheet as suggested by the seeding tables in the chapter from which you copied the draw sheet. We provide schedules for the relevant number of locations; select the appropriate one.

To use the CD, go to the file folder you are interested in and select the appropriate schedule. Click on the schedule, fill in the name of the entries, divisions, and locations, along with the dates and times of the games. Simply "tab" your way to the next field each time, and the content of the just-completed field is automatically placed in the appropriate place on the schedule. Save your file and print it to your printer or link it to a Web page.

Understanding Tournaments and Leagues

There are nine main types of tournaments or leagues described in this book: single elimination, double elimination, multilevel, straight round robin, round robin double split, round robin triple split, round robin quadruple split, semi–round robins, and extended (such as ladder and pyramid tournaments). In the passages that follow, you will find the details on each kind of tournament or league, including individual strengths and weaknesses and suggestions for the best use for each tournament and league format.

Single Elimination

The greatest appeal of the single-elimination tournament is its simplicity. Losers are eliminated, and winners advance to the next round until only one contestant remains— the tournament champion. The single-elimination tourney is valuable when the number of entries is large, time is short, and the number of locations is limited. Of all the tournaments, this one requires the fewest games (or matches); however, half the participants are eliminated after one game, and only a quarter of the participants remain after the second round. When more extensive participation is important and more locations and time are available, a single-elimination tournament is probably not your best choice. Yes, a single-elimination format is the most simple, but the other tournaments described in this manual are also easy to organize, so the simplicity of single elimination is not a significant factor in its favor.

Probably the best use for the single-elimination tournament is playoffs at the end of a season or following a longer tournament, such as a split round robin. You would then determine seeding for the single elimination by the standings at the conclusion of the previous playing period. Single-elimination tournaments are discussed in depth in chapter 2.

Double Elimination

The double-elimination tournament is designed to address two problems inherent in the single-elimination tournament. The first is that one of the best entries may have a bad first game or match or have been poorly seeded in the single-elimination draw; if that occurs in a single-elimination tournament, that entry is eliminated too soon. Having a losers' bracket gives such an entry an opportunity to play in the finals. The second problem with the single elimination is that half of the entries play only one game (or match). The double-elimination format ensures that all entries play at least two games.

However, this tournament type is often overrated because of those strengths. It also has weaknesses, and there are good alternatives. The major difficulties with the double elimination are that the second- and third-seeded players play many games, particularly in the final rounds of the tournament, and it takes many rounds to complete. Also, this tournament type often does not use available areas efficiently. For example, if the tournament consists of nine entries and there are four locations available, the double-elimination tournament takes seven rounds to complete. This is as many rounds as in a round robin double split (discussed later) but without the advantages a round robin tournament offers.

The double elimination's major benefit is for situations in which the number of locations is limited, time is at a premium, final standings are important, and all entries are to be awarded a minimum of two games. For more on double eliminations, see chapter 4.

Multilevel

The multilevel tournament is similar to a single-elimination tournament; in fact, at the top level they are the same. However, in a multilevel tournament, a player is not eliminated following a loss but simply moves down one or more levels of play into the consolation rounds. This downward movement continues until no other challengers remain. One result of this approach is that all players play about the same number of games. Another benefit is that in each round the players are more likely to encounter other players of their caliber.

In the final rounds of play in single- and double-elimination tournaments, there are only one or two locations in use. This is not the case in the multilevel tournament. As a result, when sufficient locations are available, the multilevel tournament takes the same amount of time to complete as a single-elimination tournament and half the time of a double-elimination tournament. For example, if six locations are available, and the tournament contains 13 entries, it takes four rounds to complete the tournament using either the single elimination or the multilevel and eight rounds to complete a double elimination. The multilevel tournament is an excellent choice when equality in number of games played and closely contested matches are important, when time is limited, and when knowledge of third and subsequent final placements is not crucial.

This tournament is perhaps most useful in physical education classes or intramural or recreational settings where eliminating players is undesirable and final standings are of little significance. Because this tournament type offers many advantages in these situations, and because it may be new to the reader, we advise a review of chapter 3.

Straight Round Robin

The round robin tournament and league schedules consist of all individuals or teams playing each entry an equal number of times. The round robin and round robin split schedules all have fixed schedules; all entries know exactly who they play and what time they play them, which offers some advantage to entries in preparing for the tournament and upcoming games. Seeding does not affect the outcome because the cumulative results of all games played determine final standings. When the number of entries is few and games are played quickly (as in table tennis, badminton, or volleyball), this type of format is effective for a one-day tournament. When there are more entries and the games take longer to complete (as in hockey, football, or basketball), then a round robin schedule is best suited for league play. In this case, one time through a round robin provides the league schedule, and, if time permits, you could provide a home and away schedule simply by going through the round robin schedule twice.

The round robin format is not suitable for all situations. Because all entries play each other, a round robin format is problematic when the number of entries is high. For example, a tournament with 32 entries would take 496 games to complete using a round robin. This compares with 62 games in a double elimination and 31 in single elimination. Also, when there is considerable discrepancy in caliber of play, many games or matches will prove unsatisfactory to all involved in these (non)contests. For more on the regular round robin tournament and the other round robin formats discussed in the following paragraphs, see chapter 5.

The largest number of schedules on the CD is for round robins. To help you find the schedule you want, the files have been divided into two main folders: 3–8 entries and 9–16 entries, locations shared and locations different. Within those folders, the files are further subdivided by type of round robin and by league. The league schedules have a home location. The other round robin schedules could also be used for league schedules in which entries share locations. For example, a community soccer league of 10 teams might share two soccer fields.

Round Robin Double Split

When a round robin format is desirable, but the number of entries is too large, splitting the entries into two divisions is a practical solution. Following the play within the divisions, only the top two entries from each division participate in playoffs to determine the final top standings. The obvious benefit is that the number of games is halved. The drawback is that accurate seeding becomes important. For example, if the top three seeds are placed in one division and only the top two from each division advance to the playoffs, then (if entries perform consistent with their seedings) the third seed cannot play in the playoffs.

The round robin double split is commonly used for league play. You could split the league into two or more divisions, with the playoffs bringing together the top two teams from each division to decide the final standings.

Round Robin Triple Split

The round robin triple split is similar to the double split. However, because it would be awkward to have a single-elimination playoff with three or six finalists, a round robin format for the finalists is the most suitable. This requires more games in the playoffs and is a satisfactory alternative to the double split only when there are a very large number of entries.

Round Robin Quadruple Split

This type of tournament or league is intended to solve the same problems addressed by the double split, but instead of dividing the entries into two groups, they are divided into four groups. This is useful only when the number of entries exceeds 11. You could use this format in a one- or two-day tournament or in a league over a longer time. The major disadvantage of this approach is that when there are only 12 to 15 entries, the weaker players (or teams) might participate in only two games.

Semi–Round Robins

The semi–round robin is essentially a round robin tournament but solves the problem of uneven divisions. For example, in a baseball tournament if there were seven entries divided into two divisions, one division would have three entries, and the other would have four. This means that the division with four entries requires each entry to compete in one more game than in the division with three entries. The semi–round robin corrects for this. This type of tournament is explained further in chapter 7.

Extended

Ladders and pyramids are two common examples of extended tournaments or leagues. Extended tournaments can be ongoing for an indefinite time or can be abbreviated to a week, a month, or another set period. For drop-in programs, such as intramurals or racket clubs, this tournament type can be most useful. Its major weaknesses are, first, that players challenge each other, which means that some players might not play as much, and, second, because of the challenge system the ranking at the end of the tournament might not be accurate. A round robin ladder tournament is presented in chapter 7, which combines the strengths of ladder type tournaments with the fixed scheduling of round robin schedules. We discuss extended tournaments in detail in chapter 6.

Selecting Tournament and League Type

There are five important variables to consider when planning a tournament or league: the number of games required to complete a tournament, equality of the numbers of games entries will be participating in, how long the tournament will last, how close most of the games will be, and how important accuracy of seeding is to a well-run tournament. In table 1.1, each tournament type is evaluated.

If you are pressed for time and have only one location, a single-elimination format will always be the quickest way of completing a tournament. However, if you have more playing sites available, single-elimination's time advantage is minimized. In table 1.2, we identify how many rounds it takes to complete tournaments of various sizes using a number of locations.

Various assumptions are built into these calculations. In double elimination it is assumed that the number-one seed does not lose any matches. For round robin split tournaments, the top two finishers of each division advanced to the playoffs, and we have also included a game for third and fourth place. Therefore, the playoff round requires four extra games for the double split, six extra games for the triple split, and eight games for the quadruple split.

Table 1.2 shows you the number of rounds it takes to complete a tournament, helping you weigh your tournament goals against time and facility requirements.

Table 1.1   Tournament Selection Guide

	Number of games	Equal number of games for all entries	Time to complete tournament (more than one location)	Number of nonclose games	Importance of accurate seeding
Single elimination	Very few	Very poor	Short	Many	Very important
Double elimination	Few	Poor	Long	Few	Important
Multilevel	Few	Good	Short	Very few	Very important
Round robin	Very many	Very good	Very long	Many	Not very important
Round robin double split	Many	Good	Long	Many	Important
Round robin triple split	Many	Good	Long	Many	Important
Round robin quadruple split	Few	Good	Long	Many	Important
Semi–round robin	Few	Very good	Short	Many	Important
Extended	Optional	Possible	Optional	Many	Not very important

Table 1.2 Rounds to Complete Tournament

Number of entries	Number of locations							
	1	2	3	4	5	6	7	8
Two entries								
SE	1							
Three entries								
SE	2							
DE	4							
RR	3							
Four entries								
SE	3	2						
DE	6	4						
RR	6	3						
Five entries								
SE	4	3						
DE	8	5						
RR	10	5						
Six entries								
SE	5	3	3					
ML	7	4	3					
DE	10	6	6					
RR	15	8	5					
RD	10	5	5					
Seven entries								
SE	6	4	3					
ML	9	5	3					
DE	12	7	6					
RR	21	11	7					
RD	13	7	5					
SRR	10	6	5					
Eight entries								
SE	7	4	4	3				
ML	12	6	5	3				
DE	14	8	7	6				
RR	28	14	10	7				
RD	16	8	6	5				
SRR	11	6	5	4				
Nine entries								
SE	8	5	4	4				
ML	14	7	5	4				
DE	16	9	8	7				
RR	36	18	12	9				
RD	20	10	8	7				
RT	15	8	8	8				
SRR	14	8	6	6				
Ten entries								
SE	9	5	4	4	4			
ML	15	8	5	4	4			
DE	18	10	8	7	7			
RR	45	23	15	12	9			
RD	24	12	9	7	7			
RT	15	9	7	6	6			
SRR	15	7	7	6	6			

(continued)

Table 1.2 Rounds to Complete Tournament, *continued*

Number of entries	1	2	3	4	5	6	7	8
Eleven entries								
SE	10	6	5	4	4			
ML	17	9	6	5	4			
DE	20	11	9	8	8			
RR	55	28	19	14	11			
RD	29	15	11	9	7			
RT	21	11	8	7	6			
SRR	16	9	7	6	6			
Twelve entries								
SE	11	6	5	4	4	4		
ML	20	10	7	5	5	5		
DE	22	12	10	8	8	8		
RR	66	33	17	14	11	11		
RD	34	17	12	10	8	7		
RT	24	12	9	8	7	6		
RQ	20	10	8	6	6	6		
SRR	19	10	8	6	6	6		
Thirteen entries								
SE	12	7	5	5	4	4		
ML	22	11	8	6	5	4		
DE	24	13	10	9	8	8		
RR	78	39	26	20	16	13		
RD	40	20	14	11	10	9		
RT	28	14	11	9	8	7		
RQ	23	12	9	7	6	6		
SRR	20	11	9	7	6	6		
Fourteen entries								
SE	13	8	6	5	5	4	4	
ML	25	13	9	7	5	5	4	
DE	26	14	11	9	9	8	8	
RR	91	46	31	23	19	16	13	
RD	46	23	16	13	11	9	9	
RT	32	16	12	10	9	8	8	
RQ	26	13	10	8	7	6	6	
SRR	21	11	9	7	6	6	6	
Fifteen entries								
SE	14	8	6	5	5	5	4	
ML	28	14	10	7	6	6	4	
DE	28	15	12	10	9	9	8	
RR	105	53	35	27	21	18	15	
RD	53	27	19	15	12	11	9	
RT	36	19	13	11	9	8	8	
RQ	29	15	11	9	8	7	6	
SRR	24	10	9	8	7	7	7	
Sixteen entries								
SE	15	8	6	5	5	5	5	4
ML	32	15	10	8	7	6	5	4
DE	32	17	12	10	10	9	9	8
RR	120	60	40	30	24	20	18	15
RD	60	30	21	16	14	12	10	9
RT	41	21	15	12	10	9	8	8
RQ	32	16	12	9	8	8	7	6
SRR	25	13	10	8	8	7	7	7

You can observe from the table that single-elimination and double-elimination tournaments use multiple playing sites least effectively, that the round robin split tournaments use these sites reasonably well, and that multilevel and round robin tournaments use available sites most efficiently.

Here is an example illustrating how to use table 1.2. If there were eight entries and only one location, single elimination would be the quickest format to complete. However, if you had four locations, it would take just as long to complete a single-elimination tournament as it would to complete a multilevel tournament (three rounds) and only two additional rounds to complete a round robin double split tournament (five rounds).

Establishing Seeds and Byes

Seeding and byes are important concepts to understand in preparing a successful tournament. Reading chapter 8 will help you understand how to place byes and how to seed in a variety of tournaments. The following section briefly defines seeding and byes and indicates how you can implement these concepts using this manual and the CD.

Assigning Seeds

Seeding is defined as the process of ranking players before the tournament according to their relative ability. The main principle, especially for an elimination tournament, is that the top two entries should meet in the final game; the logical extension of this is that the higher an entry is ranked, the closer it should come to the final game before being eliminated. A second principle, which is applied differently depending on the seeding philosophy, is that it should be equally difficult for entries of similar ability to achieve similar ends. Let's quickly illustrate this point with a tournament of 16 entries. Using the advantage seeding approach, the 1st seed competes with the 16th seed, and the 2nd seed competes with the 15th seed; the highest seed plays the easiest competitor, the 2nd seed plays the second easiest competitor.

Figure 1.1 illustrates how seeding works using the advantage seeding approach, showing a draw sheet for a single elimination with five entries. If all goes according to seeding, seed number five should be eliminated first because it should be the weakest entry. In the second round, the third and fourth seeds should be eliminated, and in the final round the second seed should be eliminated, leaving the top seed victorious. Figure 1.2 on page 11 illustrates ranking based on equitable seeding.

The number of rounds gives important but only partial information. It is also helpful to know how different tournament types affect the number of games each entry can expect. For example, one goal of many tournaments, especially in recreational settings, is to equalize the number of games each entry plays. Often this goal needs to be compromised because of limited playing time or the importance of determining overall rankings. The purpose of table 1.3 on page 12 is to provide data on the number of games required for eight common tournament types. This information should assist the tournament director in selecting the tournament best suited to his or her tournament goals.

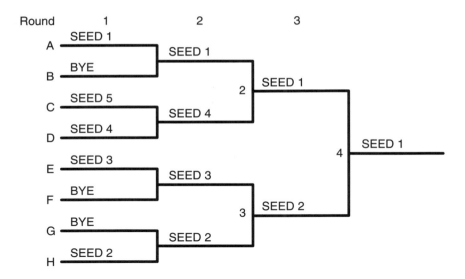

Figure 1.1   Single elimination with five entries.

A discussion of the playoff structure used to calculate the number of games for each tournament follows. The double-elimination (DE) data were calculated assuming the first-place team lost no matches. The round robin double split (RD) was calculated assuming a four-game playoff format with the top four teams. The round robin triple split (RT) was calculated assuming a 6-player round robin (RR) playoff for the top two finishers in each of the three divisions. The round robin quadruple split (RQ) was calculated assuming a single-elimination (SE), 8-entry playoff with a third- and fourth-place match. The semi–round robin (SRR) was calculated assuming a 4-entry playoff for 7 to 8 entries, a 6-entry playoff for 9 to 11 entries, an 8-entry playoff for 12 to 16 entries. The SE and RR do not have any additional playoff structure.

The following example illustrates how you can use the tables. If there were 12 entries and sufficient time, the RR would clearly be the best for equalizing the number of games played, because in the RR everyone plays the same number of games. However, the RR would require 66 games. If you want to limit the number of games, then the multilevel (ML) tournament would be the next best choice. The total number of games is decreased from 66 to 20, and the difference between the number of games played is only one, with the maximum games played being four and minimum played being three. However, one difficulty of the ML tournament is that it does not allow players who lost a match to regain their position, something that the round robin split tournament and the DE do. Of those tournament types, you would be likely to prefer the RD because the spread in the number of games played is only two, with a maximum of seven games to a minimum of five. However, this format would require 34 games. If 34 games are too many, the other four options are available. You can quickly dismiss the RT because it requires only one game less and significantly increases the spread in number of games played. The SRR is a good option because it uses the fewest games (except for the SE) and ensures two games per entry, but four of the entries will play only two games whereas two entries will play five games. For the remaining two formats, the DE is slightly better than the RQ in equalizing

Starting position	Number of entries													
	3	4	5	6	7	8	9	10	11	12	13	14	15	16
A	1	1	1	1	1	1	1	1	1	1	1	1	1	1
B	B	4	B	B	B	6	B	B	B	B	B	B	B	10
C	3	3	5	5	5	5	B	B	10	11	12	13	14	15
D	2	2	4	4	4	4	6	6	6	6	6	6	6	6
E			3	3	3	3	5	5	5	5	5	5	5	5
F			B	6	7	8	B	B	B	10	11	12	13	14
G			B	B	6	7	B	B	B	B	10	11	12	13
H			2	2	2	2	4	4	4	4	4	4	4	4
I							3	3	3	3	3	3	3	3
J							B	B	B	B	B	10	11	12
K							9	9	9	9	9	9	9	9
L							8	8	8	8	8	8	8	8
M							7	7	7	7	7	7	7	7
N							B	10	11	12	13	14	15	16
O							B	B	B	B	B	B	10	11
P							2	2	2	2	2	2	2	2

Figure 1.2 Equitable seeding for single-elimination and multilevel tournaments.

the number of games played, but the RQ requires two fewer games. Finally, if you want the fewest number of games and are not concerned that this choice would mean a format with the highest relative spread in the number of games played per entry, then the SE would be the choice. The SE requires only 11 games, but those playing in the maximum number of games play in three times as many games as those who play only one game in the entire tournament. The SE is one of the worst formats for equalizing the number of games per entries.

In addition to understanding the overall effects by looking at the total, maximum, minimum, and mean number of games played, it is also important to see who is most affected by limiting the number of games. For 12 entries, RT, SE, RQ, SRR, and DE disadvantage the low-seeded players by eliminating them early from the tournament. The RT is the most unequal, and the DE and SRR are the best of these four alternatives. The RD and ML improve the number of games in which lower seeds participate. Obviously, the RR best equalizes the number of games played because each entry plays all others.

Though equalizing the number of games is most desirable in many tournament settings, the reality of time and facility constraints often imposes adjustments to this goal. If you study table 1.3, you will understand the effect different tournament options have on the number of games each entry participates in.

Table 1.3 Seeded Position Combinations

	SE	DE	ML	RR	RD	RT	RQ	SRR
Three entries								
Seeded position 1	1	2		2				
Seeded position 2	2	4		2				
Seeded position 3	1	2		2				
Total	2.00	4.00		3.00				
Maximum	2.00	4.00		2.00				
Minimum	1.00	2.00		2.00				
Mean	1.33	2.67		2.00				
Four entries								
Seeded position 1	2	3		3				
Seeded position 2	2	4		3				
Seeded position 3	1	3		3				
Seeded position 4	1	2		3				
Total	3.00	6.00		6.00				
Maximum	2.00	4.00		3.00				
Minimum	1.00	2.00		3.00				
Mean	1.50	3.00		3.00				
Five entries								
Seeded position 1	2	3		5				
Seeded position 2	2	4		4				
Seeded position 3	1	4		4				
Seeded position 4	2	3		4				
Seeded position 5	1	2		4				
Total	4.00	8.00		10.00				
Maximum	2.00	4.00		4.00				
Minimum	1.00	2.00		4.00				
Mean	1.60	3.20		4.00				
Six entries								
Seeded position 1	2	3	2	5	4			
Seeded position 2	2	4	2	5	4			
Seeded position 3	2	5	3	5	4			
Seeded position 4	2	4	3	5	4			
Seeded position 5	1	2	2	5	2			
Seeded position 6	1	2	2	5	2			
Total	5.00	10.00	7.00	15.00	10.00			
Maximum	2.00	5.00	3.00	5.00	4.00			
Minimum	1.00	2.00	2.00	5.00	2.00			
Mean	1.67	3.33	2.33	5.00	3.33			
Seven entries								
Seeded position 1	2	3	2	6	4			4
Seeded position 2	3	5	3	6	5			4
Seeded position 3	2	5	3	6	4			3
Seeded position 4	2	4	3	6	5			3
Seeded position 5	1	2	2	6	2			2
Seeded position 6	1	3	3	6	3			2
Seeded position 7	1	2	2	6	3			2
Total	6.00	12.00	9.00	21.00	13.00			10.00
Maximum	3.00	5.00	3.00	6.00	5.00			4.00
Minimum	1.00	2.00	2.00	6.00	3.00			2.00
Mean	1.71	3.43	2.57	6.00	3.71			2.86

	SE	DE	ML	RR	RD	RT	RQ	SRR
Eight entries								
Seeded position 1	3	4	3	7	5			4
Seeded position 2	3	5	3	7	5			4
Seeded position 3	2	5	3	7	5			3
Seeded position 4	2	4	3	7	5			3
Seeded position 5	1	3	3	7	3			2
Seeded position 6	1	3	3	7	3			2
Seeded position 7	1	2	3	7	3			2
Seeded position 8	1	2	3	7	3			2
Total	7.00	14.00	12.00	28.00	16.00			11.00
Maximum	3.00	5.00	3.00	7.00	5.00			4.00
Minimum	1.00	2.00	3.00	7.00	3.00			2.00
Mean	1.75	3.50	3.00	7.00	4.00			2.75
Nine entries								
Seeded position 1	3	4	3	8	5	7		4
Seeded position 2	3	5	3	8	6	7		4
Seeded position 3	2	5	3	8	5	7		4
Seeded position 4	2	4	4	8	6	7		3
Seeded position 5	1	3	3	8	3	7		4
Seeded position 6	1	4	3	8	4	7		4
Seeded position 7	1	2	3	8	3	2		2
Seeded position 8	2	3	3	8	4	2		2
Seeded position 9	1	2	3	8	4	2		2
Total	8.00	16.00	14.00	36.00	20.00	24.00		14.00
Maximum	3.00	5.00	4.00	8.00	6.00	7.00		4.00
Minimum	1.00	2.00	3.00	8.00	3.00	3.00		2.00
Mean	1.78	3.56	3.11	8.00	4.44	5.33		3.11
Ten entries								
Seeded position 1	3	4	3	9	6	7		4
Seeded position 2	3	5	3	9	6	7		4
Seeded position 3	2	5	3	9	6	8		4
Seeded position 4	2	4	3	9	6	7		3
Seeded position 5	1	4	3	9	4	7		4
Seeded position 6	1	4	3	9	4	8		3
Seeded position 7	2	3	3	9	4	2		2
Seeded position 8	2	3	3	9	4	2		2
Seeded position 9	1	2	3	9	4	3		2
Seeded position 10	1	2	3	9	4	3		2
Total	9.00	18.00	15.00	45.00	24.00	27.00		15.00
Maximum	3.00	5.00	3.00	9.00	6.00	8.00		4.00
Minimum	1.00	2.00	3.00	9.00	4.00	2.00		2.00
Mean	1.80	3.60	3.00	9.00	4.80	5.40		3.00
Eleven entries								
Seeded position 1	3	4	3	10	6	7		4
Seeded position 2	3	5	3	10	7	8		4
Seeded position 3	2	5	3	10	6	8		4
Seeded position 4	2	4	4	10	7	7		3
Seeded position 5	1	4	3	10	4	8		4
Seeded position 6	2	5	3	10	5	8		3
Seeded position 7	2	3	3	10	4	2		2
Seeded position 8	2	4	3	10	5	3		2

(continued)

Table 1.3   Seeded Position Combinations, *continued*

	SE	DE	ML	RR	RD	RT	RQ	SRR
Seeded position 9	1	2	3	10	4	3		2
Seeded position 10	1	2	3	10	5	3		2
Seeded position 11	1	2	3	10	5	3		2
Total	10.00	20.00	17.00	55.00	29.00	30.00		16.00
Maximum	3.00	5.00	4.00	10.00	7.00	8.00		4.00
Minimum	1.00	2.00	3.00	10.00	4.00	3.00		2.00
Mean	1.82	3.64	3.09	10.00	5.27	5.45		2.91
Twelve entries								
Seeded position 1	3	4	3	11	7	8	5	5
Seeded position 2	3	5	3	11	7	8	5	5
Seeded position 3	2	5	4	11	7	8	5	4
Seeded position 4	2	4	4	11	7	8	5	4
Seeded position 5	2	5	3	11	5	8	3	3
Seeded position 6	2	5	3	11	5	8	3	3
Seeded position 7	2	4	3	11	5	3	3	3
Seeded position 8	2	4	3	11	5	3	3	3
Seeded position 9	2	4	3	11	5	3	3	2
Seeded position 10	1	2	4	11	5	3	2	2
Seeded position 11	1	2	3	11	5	3	2	2
Seeded position 12	1	2	3	11	5	3	2	2
Total	11.00	22.00	20.00	66.00	34.00	23.00	20.00	19.00
Maximum	3.00	5.00	4.00	11.00	7.00	8.00	5.00	5.00
Minimum	1.00	2.00	3.00	11.00	5.00	3.00	2.00	2.00
Mean	1.43	3.67	3.33	11.00	5.67	3.50	3.33	3.17
Thirteen entries								
Seeded position 1	3	4	3	12	7	8	5	5
Seeded position 2	3	5	3	12	8	8	5	5
Seeded position 3	2	5	4	12	7	9	5	4
Seeded position 4	3	5	4	12	8	8	6	4
Seeded position 5	2	5	4	12	5	8	3	3
Seeded position 6	2	5	3	12	6	9	3	3
Seeded position 7	2	4	3	12	5	3	3	3
Seeded position 8	2	4	3	12	6	3	4	3
Seeded position 9	1	2	3	12	5	4	2	2
Seeded position 10	1	3	4	12	6	3	2	2
Seeded position 11	1	2	4	12	5	3	2	2
Seeded position 12	1	2	3	12	6	4	3	2
Seeded position 13	1	2	3	12	6	4	3	2
Total	12.00	24.00	22.00	78.00	40.00	37.00	23.00	20.00
Maximum	3.00	5.00	4.00	12.00	8.00	9.00	6.00	5.00
Minimum	1.00	2.00	3.00	12.00	5.00	3.00	2.00	2.00
Mean	1.85	3.69	3.38	12.00	6.15	5.69	3.34	3.00
Fourteen entries								
Seeded position 1	3	4	3	13	8	8	5	5
Seeded position 2	3	5	4	13	8	9	5	5
Seeded position 3	3	6	4	13	8	9	6	4
Seeded position 4	3	5	4	13	8	8	6	4
Seeded position 5	2	5	4	13	6	9	3	3
Seeded position 6	2	5	3	13	6	9	3	3
Seeded position 7	2	4	3	13	6	3	4	3
Seeded position 8	2	4	4	13	6	4	4	3

	SE	DE	ML	RR	RD	RT	RQ	SRR
Seeded position 9	1	3	4	13	6	4	2	2
Seeded position 10	1	3	4	13	6	3	2	2
Seeded position 11	1	2	3	13	6	4	3	2
Seeded position 12	1	2	4	13	6	4	3	2
Seeded position 13	1	2	3	13	6	4	3	2
Seeded position 14	1	2	3	13	6	4	3	2
Total	13.00	26.00	25.00	91.00	46.00	41.00	26.00	21.00
Maximum	3.00	6.00	4.00	13.00	8.00	9.00	6.00	5.00
Minimum	1.00	2.00	3.00	13.00	6.00	3.00	2.00	2.00
Mean	1.86	3.71	3.57	13.00	6.57	5.86	3.71	3.00
Fifteen entries								
Seeded position 1	3	4	3	14	8	9	5	5
Seeded position 2	4	6	4	14	9	9	6	5
Seeded position 3	3	6	4	14	8	9	6	4
Seeded position 4	3	5	4	14	9	9	6	4
Seeded position 5	2	5	4	14	6	9	3	3
Seeded position 6	2	5	4	14	7	9	4	3
Seeded position 7	2	4	4	14	6	4	4	3
Seeded position 8	2	4	4	14	7	4	4	3
Seeded position 9	1	3	4	14	6	4	2	2
Seeded position 10	1	3	4	14	7	4	3	2
Seeded position 11	1	2	3	14	6	4	3	2
Seeded position 12	1	3	4	14	7	4	3	2
Seeded position 13	1	2	3	14	6	4	3	2
Seeded position 14	1	2	4	14	7	4	3	2
Seeded position 15	1	2	3	14	7	4	3	2
Total	14.00	28.00	28.00	105.00	53.00	45.00	29.00	22.00
Maximum	4.00	6.00	4.00	14.00	9.00	9.00	6.00	5.00
Minimum	1.00	2.00	3.00	14.00	6.00	4.00	3.00	2.00
Mean	1.88	3.73	3.73	14.00	7.07	6.00	3.87	2.93
Sixteen entries								
Seeded position 1	4	5	4	15	9	9	6	5
Seeded position 2	4	6	4	15	9	9	6	5
Seeded position 3	3	6	4	15	9	10	6	4
Seeded position 4	3	5	4	15	9	9	6	4
Seeded position 5	2	5	4	15	7	9	4	3
Seeded position 6	2	5	4	15	7	10	4	3
Seeded position 7	2	4	4	15	7	4	4	3
Seeded position 8	2	4	4	15	7	4	4	3
Seeded position 9	1	3	4	15	7	5	3	2
Seeded position 10	1	3	4	15	7	4	3	2
Seeded position 11	1	3	4	15	7	4	3	2
Seeded position 12	1	3	4	15	7	5	3	2
Seeded position 13	1	2	4	15	7	4	3	2
Seeded position 14	1	2	4	15	7	4	3	2
Seeded position 15	1	2	4	15	7	5	3	2
Seeded position 16	1	2	4	15	7	5	3	2
Total	15.00	30.00	32.00	120.00	60.00	50.00	32.00	23.00
Maximum	4.00	6.00	4.00	15.00	9.00	10.00	6.00	5.00
Minimum	1.00	2.00	4.00	15.00	7.00	4.00	3.00	2.00
Mean	1.88	3.75	4.00	15.00	7.50	6.25	4.00	2.50

Here is a list of the order in which the seeds were placed on the sample draw sheet, according to their starting positions, with starting positions labeled A through H:

Starting position	Entry
A	Seed 1
B	Bye
C	Seed 5
D	Seed 4
E	Seed 3
F	Bye
G	Bye
H	Seed 2

To make your work easier and reduce errors, each of the following chapters provides you with draw sheets as well as seeding charts. The CD makes it even easier because seeding is built into the schedules. The seeding chart below is basically the same as this position list, except that it provides seeding for up to 16 entries.

As tournament or league director, you should rank the entries according to the information you have available; then enter them onto the appropriate draw sheet as recommended by the seeding table. There might be upsets, but at least you know you have done your best to ensure a good tournament.

Scheduling Byes

A bye occurs when there are fewer players than spaces on the tournament draw, and the top-ranked players do not play anyone in the first round. In figure 1.1, the top-ranked entries do not play anyone in the first round but automatically advance to the second round; they all receive a bye. Meanwhile, the fourth- and fifth-seeded entries play each other to see which one will advance to the second round. Byes are further explained in chapter 8.

Using the Draw Sheets

Before we look at the individual tournaments, it will be helpful to briefly explain the numbers used in figure 1.1 and in the example below. The numbers on the draw sheet indicate the game numbers. In other words, game number 1 involves seed 4 playing seed 5; game number 2 involves seed 2 playing seed 3, and so on. The playing schedule in the example below indicates which games should be played when. Game 1 is played first, followed by games 2 and 3, and concluding with game 4. Schedules for the relevant number of locations are provided, and the appropriate one should be selected.

Playing schedule

(Five entries, two locations)

Location I	1	3	4
Location II	2		

Once you have decided which tournament or league type to use, you will notice how easy it is to assign entries to a draw sheet and schedule your competition. You are on your way to implementing a successful tournament or league.

Assigning Game Numbers and Locations

The game numbers on the brackets for single-elimination, double-elimination, and multilevel tournaments were assigned with the assumption that there is one location to compete on. There are a couple of principles used to assign game numbers. The first principle is that game numbers should be as equally spread out as possible for each entry. The second principle is that the higher seeds are given extra space when it is not possible to spread the games out equally. The extra space is to provide extra rest because they will compete in more contests in single- and double-elimination tournaments. In the example in figure 1.3, you will notice that seed 1 is off for three games (or matches) before competing in game 5; seed 2 also has three games off. Seed 3 has only one game off, as does seed 4. You will notice that in the next round, seed 1 has one game off, and seed 2 proceeds immediately to the next game. It was not possible to give each seed an equal time off between games, thus the higher seed gains a slight advantage.

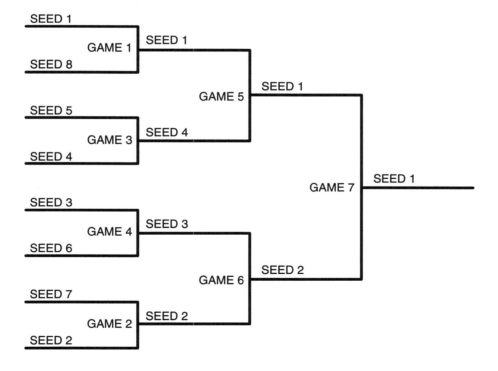

Figure 1.3 Assigning games and locations.

If we numbered the games 1 through 4 in order for each round, then seed 1 would compete in games 1 and 5, and seed 2 would compete in games 4 and 6. Seed 1 would have three games off, and seed 2 would have only one. For entries of a similar caliber, assigning game numbers in such a fashion would be unnecessarily disadvantageous to seed 2.

If there are two or more locations, the same principles apply regarding the number of games off. In the example, games 1 and 2 are played first, then games 3 and 4, then games 5 and 6, and then the championship game. Seeds 1 and 2 both get a game off; the lower seeds (3 and 4) do not.

If there are two or more locations, then the locations need to be assigned to each game. If all the locations are identical, then it does not matter which location an entry is assigned. However, locations often differ slightly. For our purposes in this book and CD, location 1 is always the superior location, followed by location 2, then location 3, and so on. How do you decide which seeds are assigned to which location? There are two principles. The first principle for assigning locations is that the closer the seeds, the better the location. The second principle is that if seeds are an equal distance apart, the higher seed gets the better location.

In the example, using two locations, the order of games is as follows:

Location I	2	3	6	7
Location II		1	4	5

Game 2 is between seed 7 and seed 2, which is a difference of 5; game 1 is between seed 8 and seed 1, which is a difference of 7. Thus, game 2 is assigned the best location. The only exception to this rule is when there is a large tournament in which seed 16 might be competing against seed 14 (a difference of two) and seed 4 might be competing at the same time against seed 1 (a difference of three). If a number of locations are available, and the tournament is in the last two rounds, then seed 1 and seed 4 would get the preferred location over seeds 14 and 16. A tournament scheduling grid is supplied to post with the tournament brackets so participants know when and where their next game is. The home team should be determined by assigning the higher seeded team as the home team or by a coin toss or other predetermined means (you can see the home team designation on the brackets as indicated by the letter "h" on the draw sheets). The software that goes with this book calculates all these details automatically. Use the tournament schedule on page 19 to write in all the games, locations, dates, and times.

Tournament Schedule

Game	Location	Date	Time
1			
2			
3			
4			
5			
6			
7			
8			
9			
10			
11			
12			
13			
14			
15			
16			
17			
18			
19			
20			
21			
22			
23			
24			
25			
26			
27			
28			
29			
30			
31			
32			

CHAPTER 2

Single-Elimination Tournaments

Implementing the single-elimination tournament is straightforward. Once you have seeded the players (or teams), enter their names on the draw sheets as suggested by the seeding tables. Then select the appropriate schedule, and play can get under way. Place the name of each player or team who wins on the draw sheet to the right of the player's or team's previously recorded game. Those who lose are eliminated from play and do not advance.

A common option to consider for ending a single-elimination tournament is to have the semifinal losers play each other. This consolation game or match, which determines third place overall, gives the first- and second-place teams a one-game break before playing their championship game. Many national and international competitions include consolation games.

The procedure for large, single-elimination tournaments is the same for small ones. If you have more than 16 entries (for example, let's say you have 32), it's best to seed them into four single-elimination draw sheets of eight entries each. The winner of these draws are then placed in a predetermined manner on a final draw sheet of four entries. If you have 64 entries, you might select four draw sheets of 16 entries or eight draw sheets of eight entries, with the winner progressing to a final draw sheet of either four or eight entries, respectively. For other options in managing a large number of entries, see chapter 7. Note, the "h" on the schedules and draw sheets denotes the home team if one is desired. Figure 2.1 shows a single-elimination bracket with eight entries.

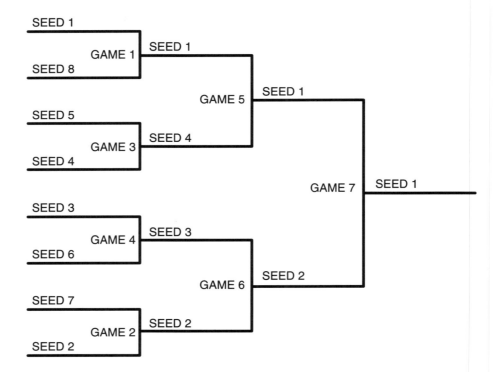

Figure 2.1 Single elimination with eight entries.

In a single-elimination tournament, here is the simple equation for determining the number of games (or matches) played:

$$\text{Number of entries} - 1 = \text{number of games}$$

Advantages of a Single-Elimination Tournament

- The format is easy to understand.
- A large number of entries can be accommodated.
- Fewer games are required.
- Few locations are required.

Disadvantages of a Single-Elimination Tournament

- Each entrant is guaranteed only one game.
- Accurate seeding is very important.
- Use of multiple locations is not maximized.

The single-elimination format is best used for end-of-the-season playoffs or following a long tournament. Figures 2.2 and 2.3 show seeding for up to 16 entries in advantage and equitable single-elimination and multilevel tournaments.

Starting position	Number of entries													
	3	4	5	6	7	8	9	10	11	12	13	14	15	16
A	1	1	1	1	1	1	1	1	1	1	1	1	1	1
B	B	4	B	B	B	8	B	B	B	B	B	B	B	16
C	3	3	5	5	5	5	9	9	9	9	9	9	9	9
D	2	2	4	4	4	4	8	8	8	8	8	8	8	8
E			3	3	3	3	5	5	5	5	5	5	5	5
F			B	6	6	6	B	B	B	12	12	12	12	12
G			B	B	7	7	B	B	B	B	13	13	13	13
H			2	2	2	2	4	4	4	4	4	4	4	4
I							3	3	3	3	3	3	3	3
J							B	B	B	B	B	14	14	14
K							B	B	11	11	11	11	11	11
L							6	6	6	6	6	6	6	6
M							7	7	7	7	7	7	7	7
N							B	10	10	10	10	10	10	10
O							B	B	B	B	B	B	15	15
P							2	2	2	2	2	2	2	2

Figure 2.2 Advantage seeding for single- and double-elimination tournaments.

Starting position	Number of entries												
	4	5	6	7	8	9	10	11	12	13	14	15	16
A	1	1	1	1	1	1	1	1	1	1	1	1	1
B	4	B	B	B	6	B	B	B	B	B	B	B	10
C	3	5	5	5	5	B	B	10	11	12	13	14	15
D	2	4	4	4	4	6	6	6	6	6	6	6	6
E		3	3	3	3	5	5	5	5	5	5	5	5
F		B	6	7	8	B	B	B	10	11	12	13	14
G		B	B	6	7	B	B	B	B	10	11	12	13
H		2	2	2	2	4	4	4	4	4	4	4	4
I						3	3	3	3	3	3	3	3
J						B	B	B	B	B	10	11	12
K						9	9	9	9	9	9	9	9
L						8	8	8	8	8	8	8	8
M						7	7	7	7	7	7	7	7
N						B	10	11	12	13	14	15	16
O						B	B	B	B	B	B	10	11
P						2	2	2	2	2	2	2	2

Figure 2.3 Equitable seeding for single-elimination and multilevel tournaments.

Using the Software

1. Open the Single Elimination folder.
2. Select your seeding method (advantage or equitable).
3. Select your file by the number of entries and number of locations. For example, SE 04E AD 2L is single elimination, four entries, advantage seeding, two locations (see figure 2.4 below).
4. Fill in the competition name, competition date, seeds, locations, dates, and times. *Note:* When completing these fields, be sure to "tab" to the next entry; doing so enters the field onto the draw sheet. If you fail to push the tab button, the field will not be entered.
5. Save the file to your hard drive.
6. Print a copy.

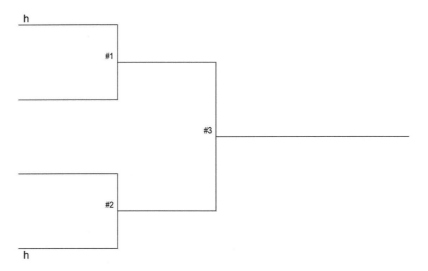

Figure 2.4   Sample single-elimination bracket for four entries, advantage seeding, with two locations.

Single-elimination tournament with 3 entries

Round   1   2

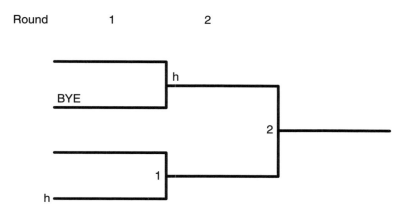

From *Organizing Successful Tournaments* (3e) by John Byl, 2006, Champaign, IL: Human Kinetics.

Single-elimination tournament with 4 entries

Round   1   2

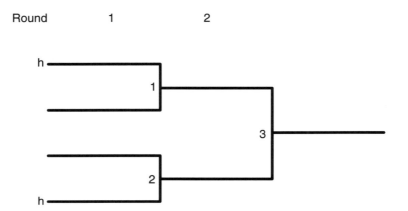

From *Organizing Successful Tournaments* (3e) by John Byl, 2006, Champaign, IL: Human Kinetics.

Single-elimination tournament with 5 entries

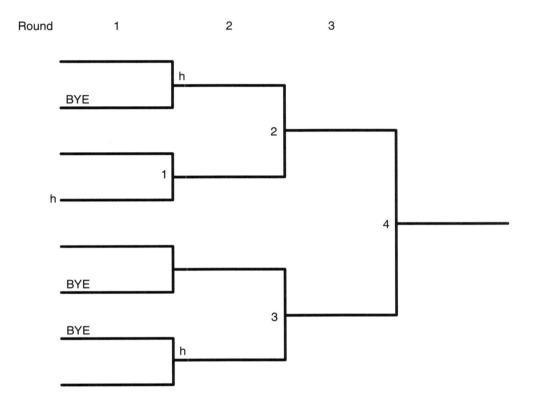

Single-elimination tournament with 6 entries

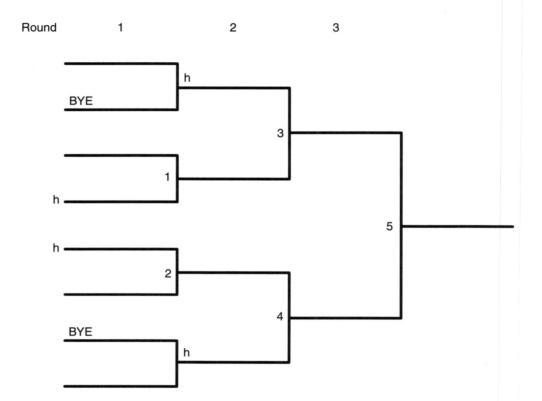

Round   1   2   3

From *Organizing Successful Tournaments* (3e) by John Byl, 2006, Champaign, IL: Human Kinetics.

Single-elimination tournament with 7 entries

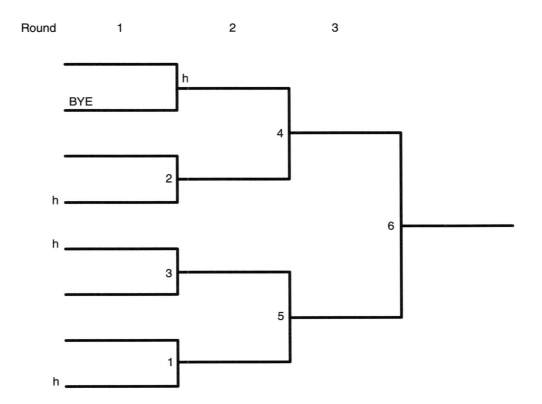

Round   1   2   3

From *Organizing Successful Tournaments* (3e) by John Byl, 2006, Champaign, IL: Human Kinetics.

Single-elimination tournament with 8 entries

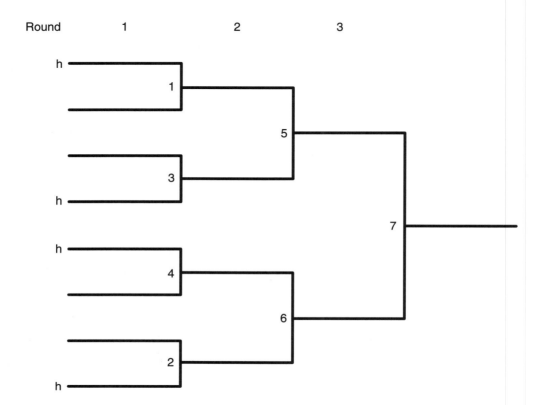

Round   1   2   3

From *Organizing Successful Tournaments* (3e) by John Byl, 2006, Champaign, IL: Human Kinetics.

Single-elimination tournament with 9 entries

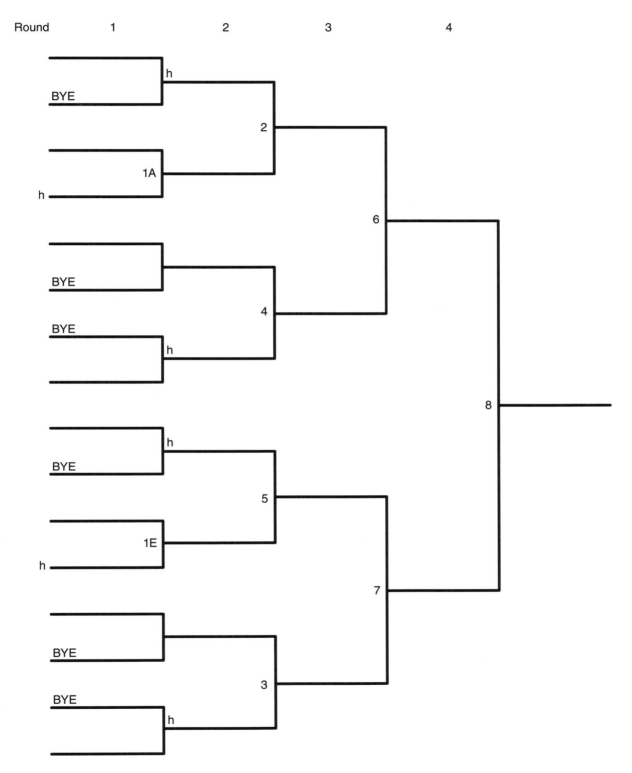

Note: One BYE needs to be added—choose your preferred seeding method and place the BYE as suggested by the respective seeding chart (on page 24).

From *Organizing Successful Tournaments* (3e) by John Byl, 2006, Champaign, IL: Human Kinetics.

Single-elimination tournament with 10 entries

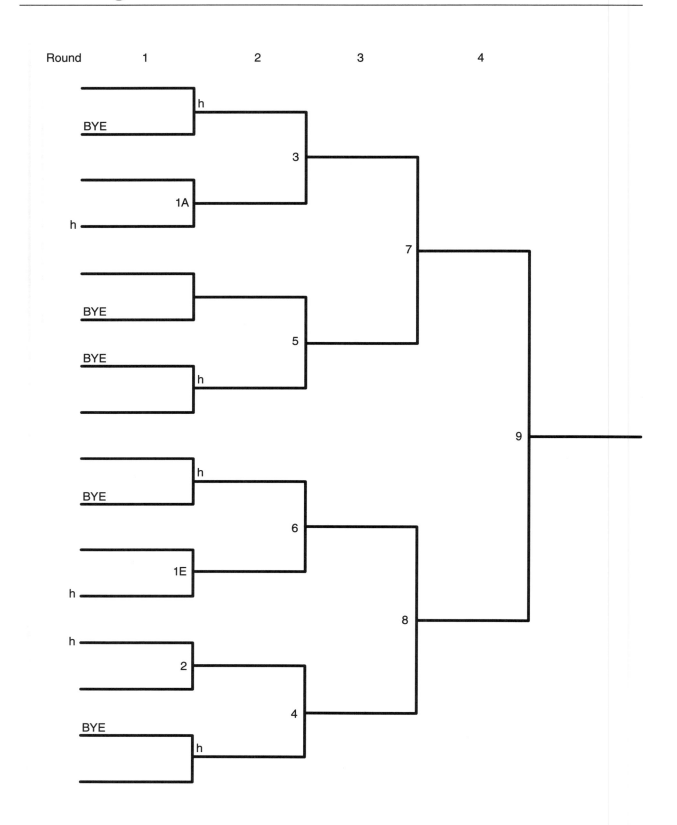

From *Organizing Successful Tournaments* (3e) by John Byl, 2006, Champaign, IL: Human Kinetics.

Single-elimination tournament with 11 entries

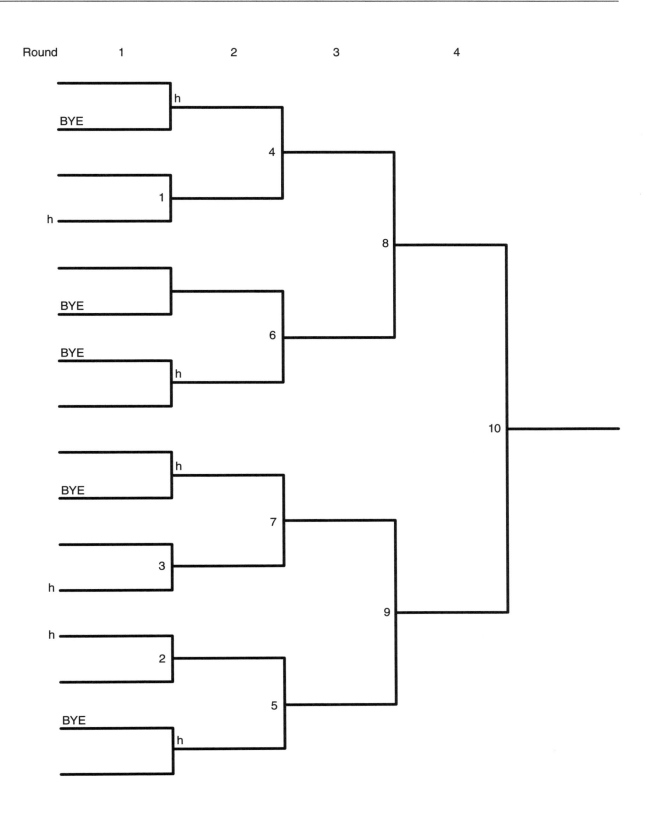

From *Organizing Successful Tournaments* (3e) by John Byl, 2006, Champaign, IL: Human Kinetics.

Single-elimination tournament with 12 entries

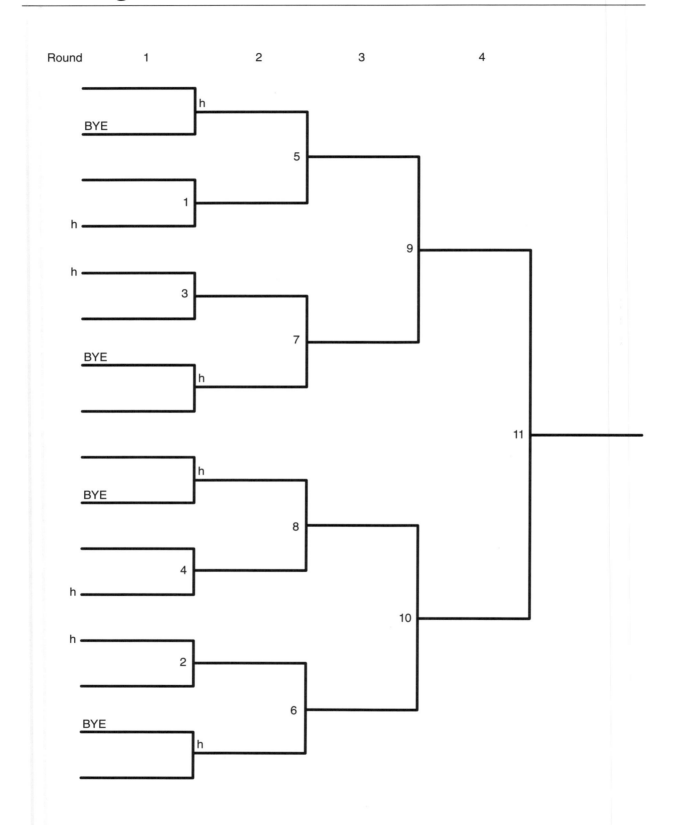

From *Organizing Successful Tournaments* (3e) by John Byl, 2006, Champaign, IL: Human Kinetics.

Single-elimination tournament with 13 entries

Round   1   2   3   4

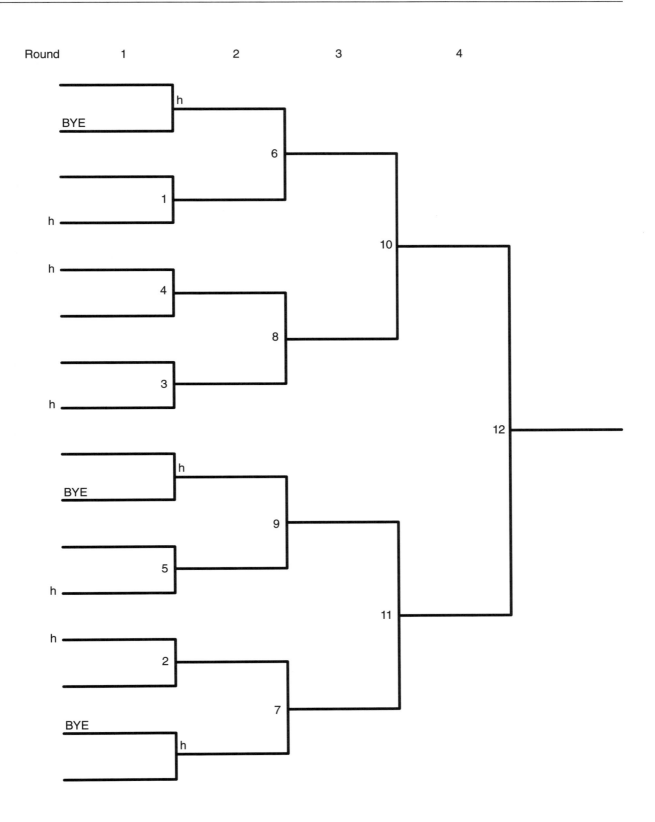

From *Organizing Successful Tournaments* (3e) by John Byl, 2006, Champaign, IL: Human Kinetics.

Single-elimination tournament with 14 entries

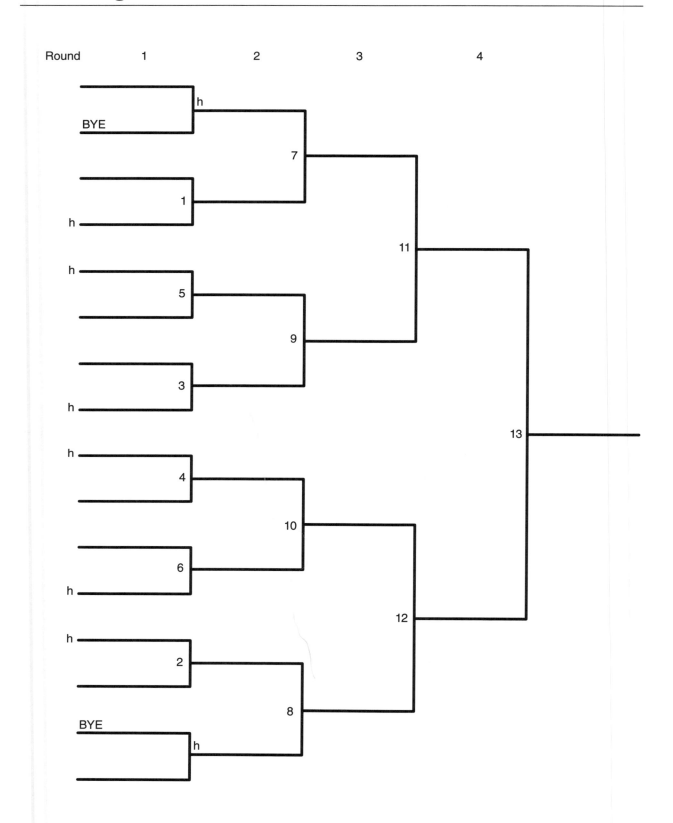

From *Organizing Successful Tournaments* (3e) by John Byl, 2006, Champaign, IL: Human Kinetics.

Single-elimination tournament with 15 entries

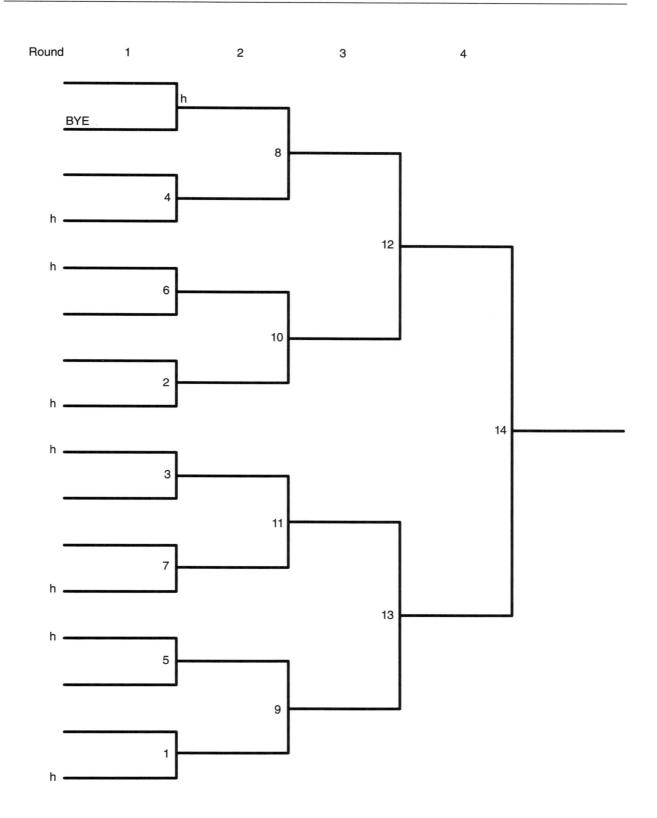

Round   1   2   3   4

From *Organizing Successful Tournaments* (3e) by John Byl, 2006, Champaign, IL: Human Kinetics.

Single-elimination tournament with 16 entries

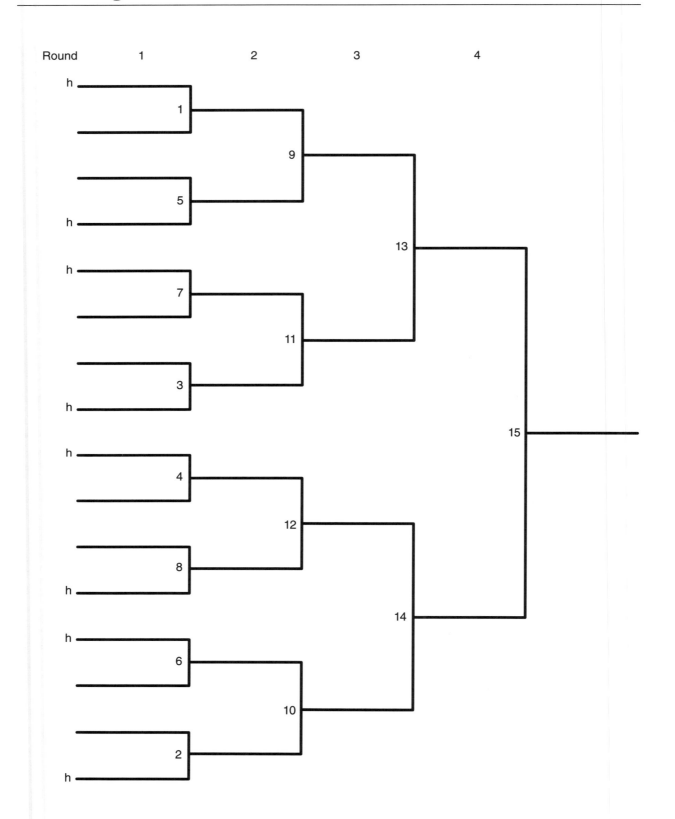

From *Organizing Successful Tournaments* (3e) by John Byl, 2006, Champaign, IL: Human Kinetics.

Playing Schedules

THREE ENTRIES

One Location

L I	1	2

FOUR ENTRIES

Two Locations

L I	2	3
L II	1	

FIVE ENTRIES

Two Locations

L I	1	3	4
L II		2	

SIX ENTRIES

Two Locations

L I	1	4	5
L II	2	3	

SEVEN ENTRIES

Two Locations

L I	1	2	5	6	1	2	5	6
L II		3	4			3	4	

Three Locations

L I	2	5	6	1	5	6
L II	3	4		2	4	
L III	1			3		

EIGHT ENTRIES

Two Locations

L I	1	3	6	7	1	3	6	7
L II	2	4	5		2	4	5	

Three Locations (same as Two Locations)

Four Locations

L I	3	6	7	3	6	7
L II	4	5		1	5	
L III	1			2		
L IV	2			4		

Playing Schedules

ADVANTAGE SEEDING *EQUITABLE SEEDING*

NINE ENTRIES

Two Locations

L I	1	2	4	7	8		1	2	4	7	8
L II		3	5	6				3	5	6	

Three Locations

L I	4	2	7	8		1	4	7	8
L II	1	3	6			2	5	6	
L III	5					3			

Four Locations

L I	1	4	7	8		1	4	7	8
L II		5	6				2	6	
L III		3					3		
L IV		2					5		

---

10 ENTRIES

Two Locations

L I	1	3	5	8	9		2	3	5	8	9
L II	2	4	6	7			1	4	6	7	

Three Locations

L I	5	6	8	9		2	5	8	9
L II	1	3	7			1	3	7	
L III	2	4				4	6		

Four Locations

L I	1	5	8	9		2	5	8	9
L II	2	6	7			1	3	7	
L III		3					4		
L IV		4					6		

---

11 ENTRIES

Two Locations

L I	1	3	4	6	9	10	3	1	4	6	9	10
L II		2	5	7	8			2	5	7	8	

Three Locations

L I	1	4	6	9	10		3	4	6	9	10
L II	3	5	7	8			1	5	7	8	
L III	2						2				

Four Locations

L I	1	6	9	10		3	6	9	10
L II	2	7	8			1	4	8	
L III	3	4				2	5		
L IV		5					7		

Playing Schedules

	ADVANTAGE SEEDING	EQUITABLE SEEDING

12 ENTRIES

Two Locations

	ADVANTAGE SEEDING	EQUITABLE SEEDING
L I	1 4 5 7 10 11	1 4 5 7 10 11
L II	2 3 6 8 9	2 3 6 8 9

Three Locations

	ADVANTAGE SEEDING	EQUITABLE SEEDING
L I	4 8 7 10 11	4 5 7 10 11
L II	3 1 5 9	1 6 8 9
L III	2 6	2 3

Four Locations

	ADVANTAGE SEEDING	EQUITABLE SEEDING
L I	1 7 10 11	4 7 10 11
L II	2 8 9	3 5 9
L III	4 5	1 6
L IV	3 6	2 8

13 ENTRIES

Two Locations

	ADVANTAGE SEEDING	EQUITABLE SEEDING
L I	3 1 4 6 8 11 12	3 1 5 6 8 11 12
L II	2 5 7 9 10	2 4 7 9 10

Three Locations

	ADVANTAGE SEEDING	EQUITABLE SEEDING
L I	1 5 8 11 12	3 5 8 11 12
L II	2 6 7 10	1 6 7 10
L III	3 4 9	2 4 9

Four Locations

	ADVANTAGE SEEDING	EQUITABLE SEEDING
L I	1 5 8 11 12	3 5 8 11 12
L II	2 6 7 10	4 6 10
L III	3 4 9	1 7
L IV		2 9

Five Locations

	ADVANTAGE SEEDING	EQUITABLE SEEDING
L I	1 8 11 12	5 8 11 12
L II	2 9 10	3 6 10
L III	5 6	4 7
L IV	4 7	1 9
L V	3	2

14 ENTRIES

Two Locations

	ADVANTAGE SEEDING	EQUITABLE SEEDING
L I	1 3 6 7 9 12 13	1 4 6 7 9 12 13
L II	2 4 5 8 10 11	2 3 5 8 10 11

Three Locations

	ADVANTAGE SEEDING	EQUITABLE SEEDING
L I	1 6 7 9 12 13	4 6 7 9 12 13
L II	2 3 8 10 11	1 3 8 10 11
L III	5 4	2 5

Playing Schedules

ADVANTAGE SEEDING   **EQUITABLE SEEDING**

Four Locations

L I	3	1	9	12	13
L II	4	2	10	11	
L III		6	7		
L IV		5	8		

L I	1	6	9	12	13
L II	2	4	7	11	
L III		3	8		
L IV		5	10		

Five Locations (same as Four Locations)

Six Locations

L I	1	9	12	13
L II	2	10	11	
L III	6	7		
L IV	5	8		
L V	4			
L VI	3			

L I	6	9	12	13
L II	4	7	11	
L III	3	8		
L IV	5	10		
L V	1			
L VI	2			

15 ENTRIES

Two Locations (same for Advantage and Equitable Seeding)

L I	1	4	3	7	9	10	13	14
L II	5	2	6	8	11	12		

Three Locations

L I	4	5	7	10	13	14
L II	1	2	8	11	12	
L III	6	3	9			

L I	1	3	7	10	13	14
L II	4	2	8	11	12	
L III	5	6	9			

Four Locations

L I	4	7	10	13	14
L II	5	6	11	12	
L III	1	2	8		
L IV		3	9		

L I	1	7	10	13	14
L II	4	3	8	12	
L III	5	2	9		
L IV		6	11		

Five Locations (same as Four Locations)

Six Locations (same as Four Locations)

Seven Locations

L I	4	10	13	14
L II	5	11	12	
L III	7	9		
L IV	6	8		
L V	2			
L VI	3			
L VII	1			

L I	7	10	13	14
L II	1	8	12	
L III	3	9		
L IV	2	11		
L V	6			
L VI	4			
L VII	5			

Playing Schedules

ADVANTAGE SEEDING	EQUITABLE SEEDING

16 ENTRIES

Two Locations (same for Advantage and Equitable Seeding)

L I	2	5	3	8	9	11	14	15
L II	1	6	4	7	10	12	13	

Three Locations

L I	5	6	8	11	14	15		1	4	8	11	14	15
L II	2	3	9	12	13			2	5	9	10	13
L III	1	4	7	10				3	6	7	12	

(Advantage: L I: 5 6 8 11 14 15; L II: 2 3 9 12 13; L III: 1 4 7 10)
(Equitable: L I: 1 4 8 11 14 15; L II: 2 5 9 10 13; L III: 3 6 7 12)

Four Locations

Advantage:
L I	5	8	11	14	15
L II	6	7	12	13	
L III	2	3	9		
L IV	1	4	10		

Equitable:
L I	1	8	11	14	15
L II	2	4	9	13
L III	5	3	10	
L IV	6	7	12	

Five Locations (same as Four Locations)

Six Locations (same as Four Locations)

Seven Locations (same as Four Locations)

Eight Locations

Advantage:
L I	5	11	14	15
L II	6	12	13	
L III	8	9		
L IV	7	10		
L V	3			
L VI	4			
L VII	2			
L VIII	1			

Equitable:
L I	8	11	14	15
L II	1	9	13	
L III	2	10		
L IV	4	12		
L V	3			
L VI	7			
L VII	5			
L VIII	6			

CHAPTER 3

Multilevel Tournaments

We can best understand the multilevel tournament as a single-elimination tournament with many consolation rounds. The intent of the multilevel format is threefold: to avoid eliminating participants who lose, to provide as many closely contested games as possible, and to complete all play within a reasonable time limit.

It is perhaps best to explain this kind of tournament by taking you through an example of a multilevel, eight-entry tournament, as shown in figure 3.1 (see page 47). The top bracket is much the same as in a single-elimination tournament, seeding players (or teams) according to the equitable seeding chart (page 11) and placing the name of each winner on the line to the right of that player's or team's previous game (or match). The entry who progresses to the far right of the draw sheet without losing comes in first in section A (and thus first overall). The entry defeated last by the first-place entry would be in second place. However, unlike single elimination, in which half the entries for the tournament are eliminated after the first round of play, those who lose in the first round drop to section C and play in round 2 at that level. With respect to the goals of this tournament type, those who lose continue to play, and all entries will be playing someone close to their ability level in this round. Following the second round, those who lose in section A drop to section B, and those who lose in section C drop to section D. Once again, no entry is eliminated from the tournament, and all entries play someone close in ability in the final round.

The advantages of this type of tournament are obvious. First, all entries play approximately the same number of games. Second, the similarity in the level of play is close in round 2 and even closer in round 3; in other words, each round sees entries playing others of more similar ability, which usually makes for the most satisfying games. The multilevel tournament takes less time than double elimination because it requires fewer games (or matches). Considering these advantages, the multilevel tournament is well worth considering. However, as in single elimination, precise seeding is important. In a setup such as the one shown in figure 3.1, those who lose in the first round can do no better than fifth place overall; this is the major disadvantage of the multilevel tournament. Considering the advantages and disadvantages, you can see why this tournament is well suited to physical education classes or intramural settings in which equality of playing time is important.

For a multilevel tournament involving more than 16 entries, there are two possible solutions. The first is to divide the entries into two pools, each playing in a multilevel format, and then have a playoff for the A-level players or the A- and B-level players. A second option, one that is more time consuming, is to prepare one multilevel tournament including all the entries. To limit the length of play, limit the levels to four (note that this changes the number of games per entry). Limiting the levels to four ensures all entries of participating in at least three games. You could prepare level A using the single-elimination draw sheets and seeding tables in chapter 2. Those who lose in the first round would play in level C, a single-elimination draw suitable for a group half the size of level A. Those who lose in the second round would drop one level—those in level A drop to level B, those in C drop to D. In the third and subsequent rounds, a player would be eliminated from further play following a loss. You could draw the B to D levels using single-elimination draw sheets as well. Again, the "h" denotes the home entry if desired.

Advantages of a Multilevel Tournament

- All entrants play approximately the same number of games.
- There are few lopsided games because each round has entries competing with others of more similar abilities.
- Fewer games are required.
- You can use multiple locations effectively.
- Each entrant plays more games than he or she would in a single- or double-elimination format.

Disadvantages of a Multilevel Tournament

- Round 1 losers rank in the bottom half of entries.
- Accurate seeding is crucial.

The multilevel tournament is best used in classes and intramural or recreational settings in which eliminating entrants is undesirable and standings are not crucial.

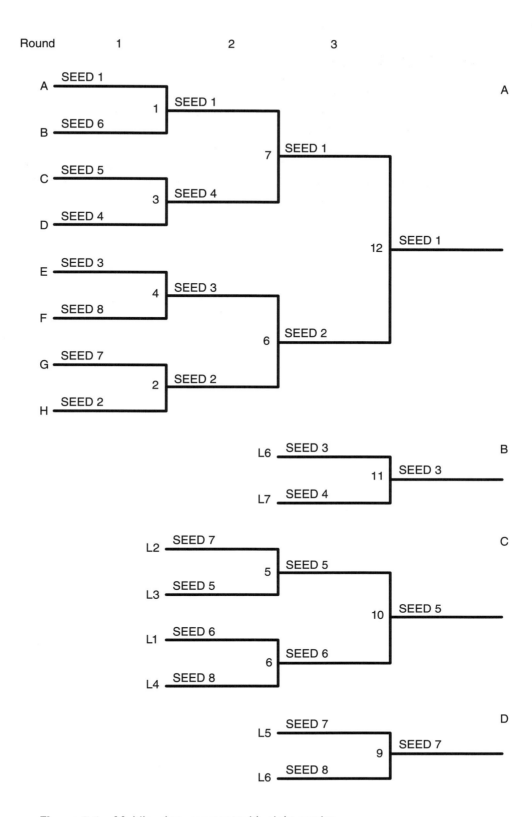

Figure 3.1 Multilevel tournament with eight entries.

Using the Software

1. Open the Multilevel folder.
2. Select your number of entries and locations. For example, ML 5E 2L is multilevel, 5 entries, 2 locations (see figure 3.2).
3. Fill in the competition name, competition date, seeds, locations, dates, and times. *Note:* When completing these fields, be sure to tab to the next entry; doing so enters the field onto the draw sheet. If you fail to push the tab button, the field will not be entered.
4. Save the file to your hard drive.
5. Print a copy.

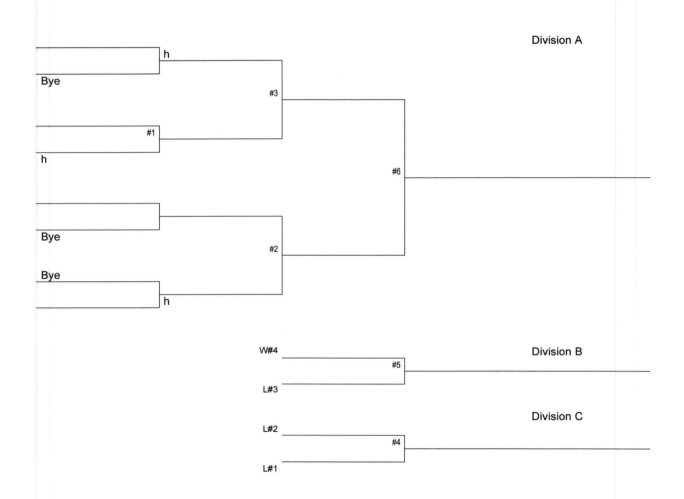

Figure 3.2   Sample multilevel bracket with five entries and two locations.

Multilevel tournament with 4 entries

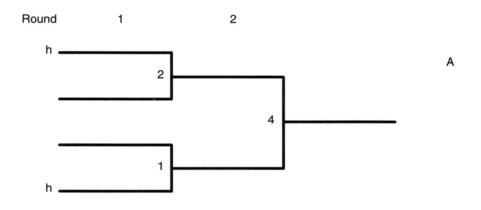

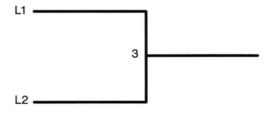

From *Organizing Successful Tournaments* (3e) by John Byl, 2006, Champaign, IL: Human Kinetics.

Multilevel tournament with 5 entries

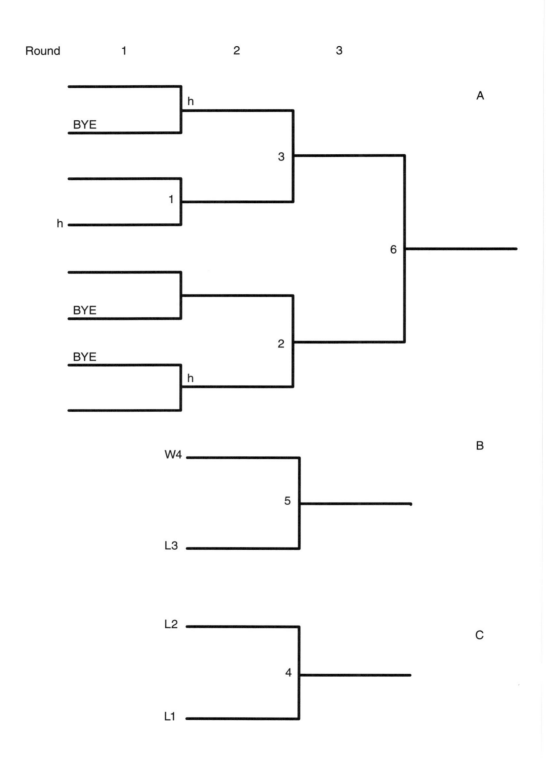

From *Organizing Successful Tournaments* (3e) by John Byl, 2006, Champaign, IL: Human Kinetics.

Multilevel tournament with 6 entries

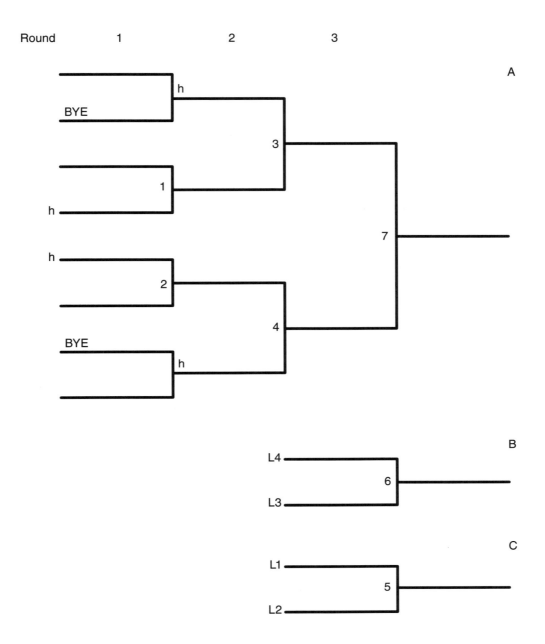

Multilevel tournament with 7 entries

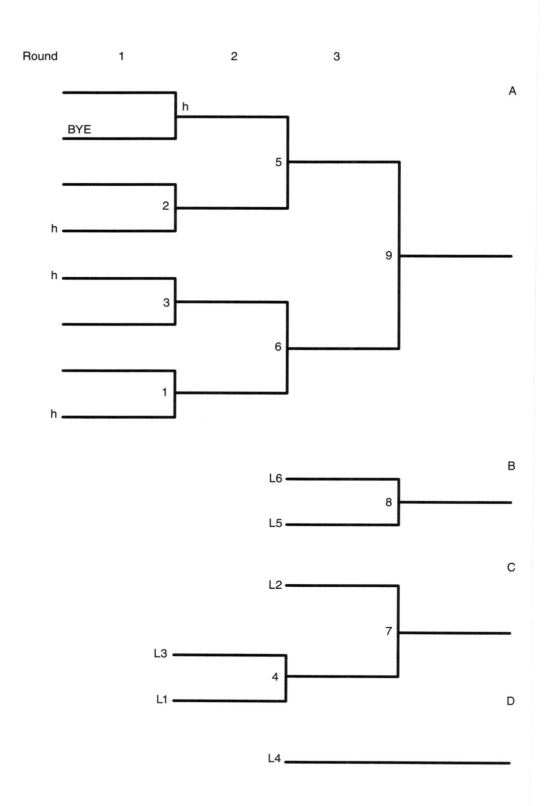

Multilevel tournament with 8 entries

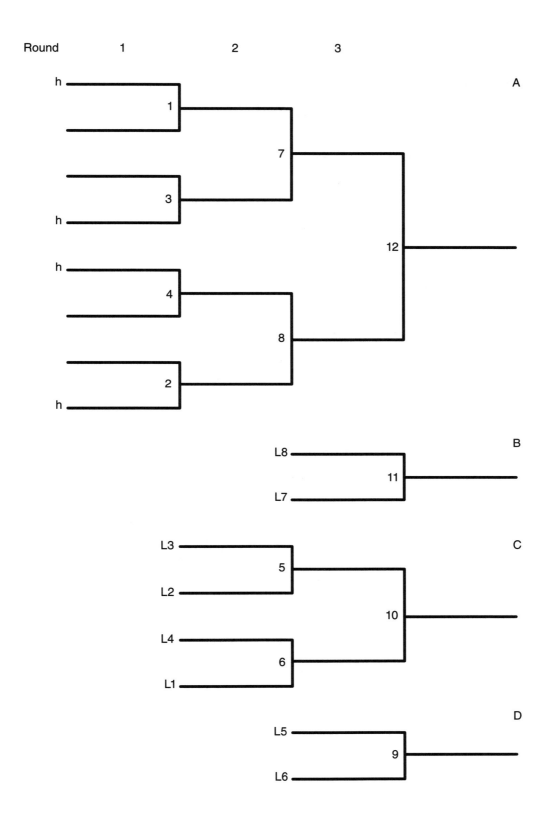

Multilevel tournament with 9 entries

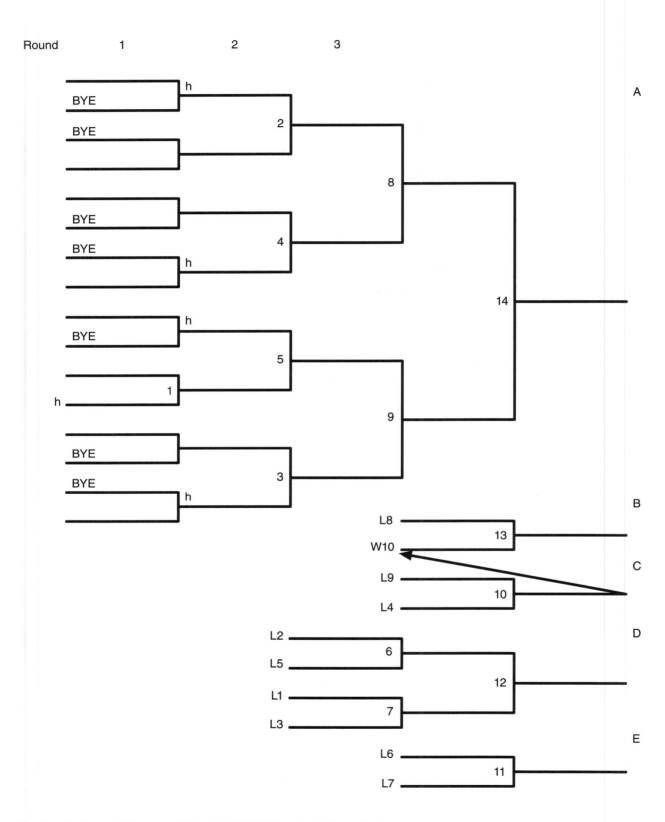

From *Organizing Successful Tournaments* (3e) by John Byl, 2006, Champaign, IL: Human Kinetics.

Multilevel tournament with 10 entries

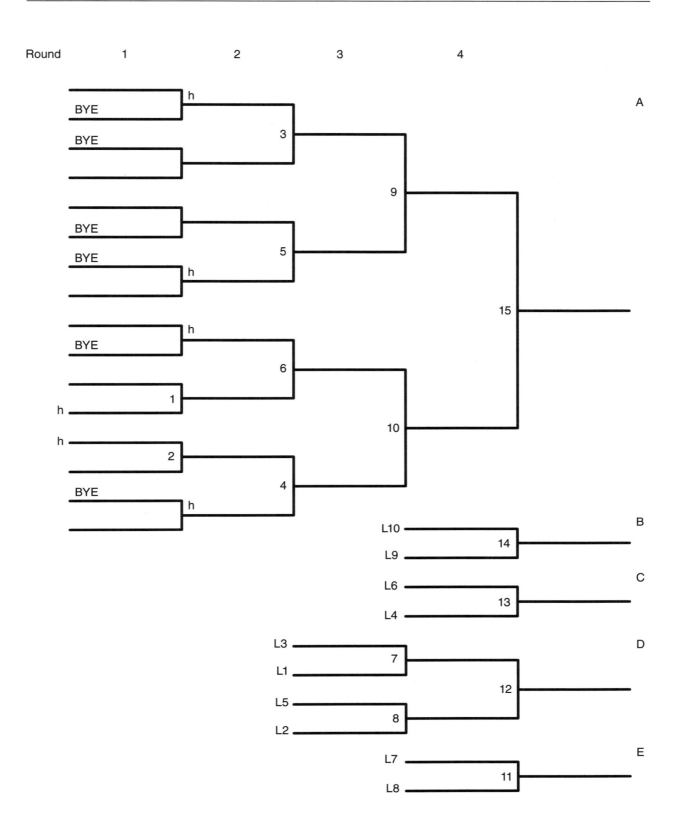

From *Organizing Successful Tournaments* (3e) by John Byl, 2006, Champaign, IL: Human Kinetics.

Multilevel tournament with 11 entries

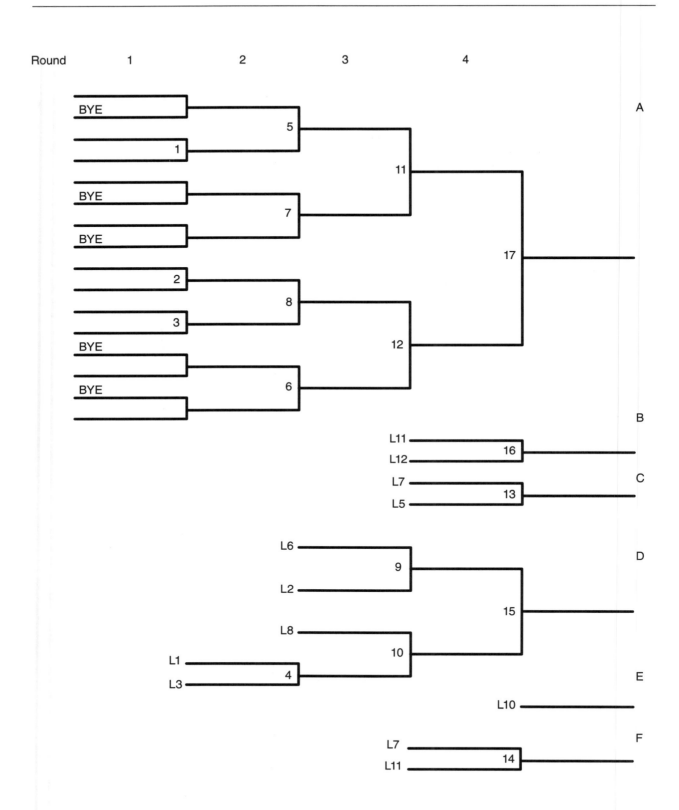

From *Organizing Successful Tournaments* (3e) by John Byl, 2006, Champaign, IL: Human Kinetics.

Multilevel tournament with 12 entries

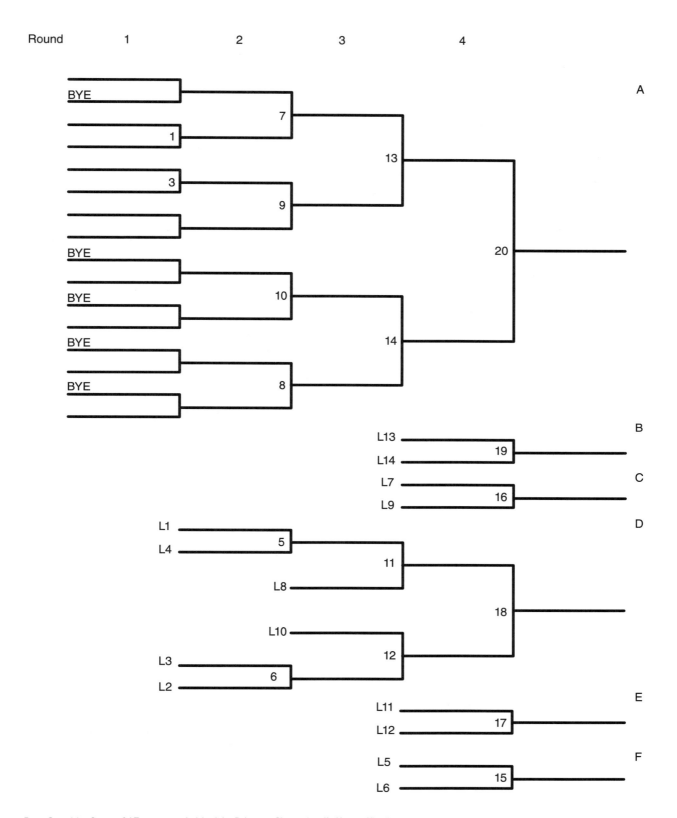

From *Organizing Successful Tournaments* (3e) by John Byl, 2006, Champaign, IL: Human Kinetics.

Multilevel tournament with 13 entries

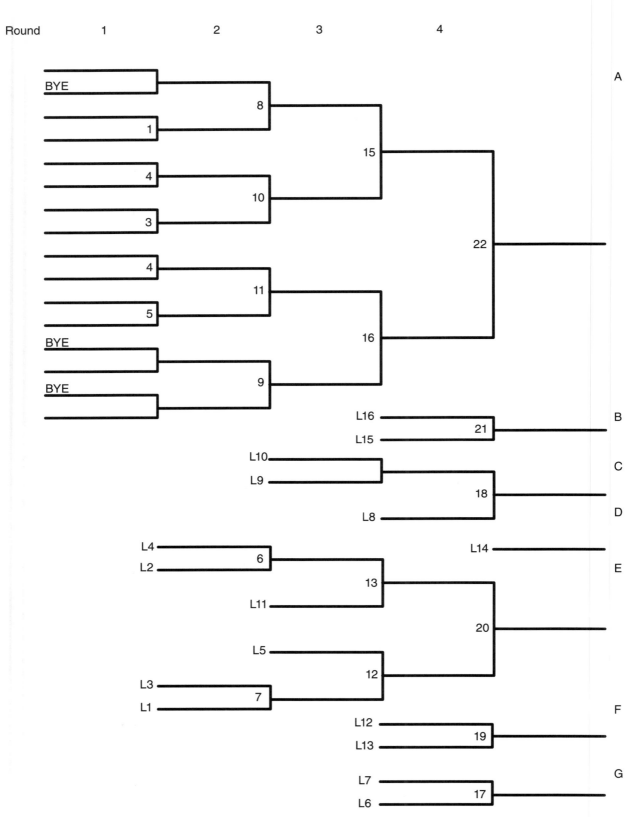

From *Organizing Successful Tournaments* (3e) by John Byl, 2006, Champaign, IL: Human Kinetics.

Multilevel tournament with 14 entries

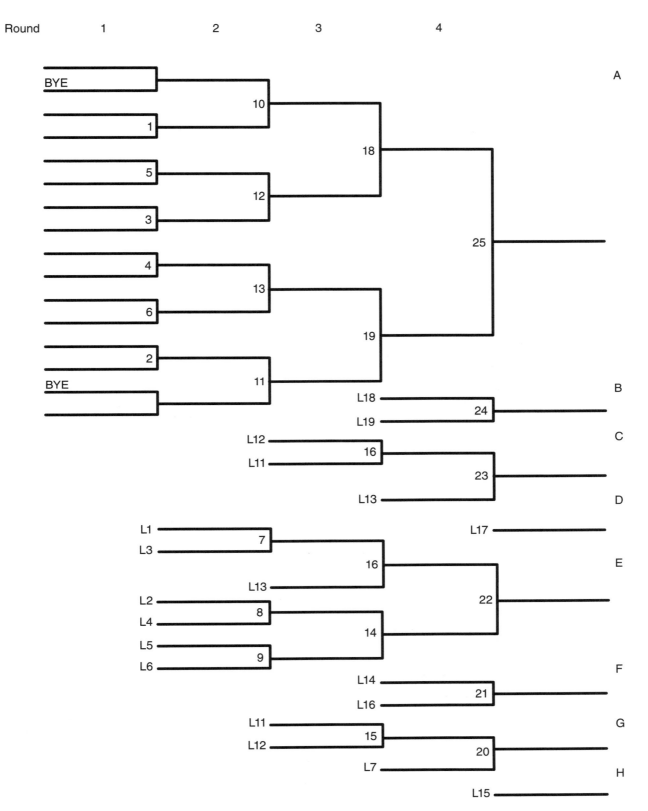

Multilevel tournament with 15 entries

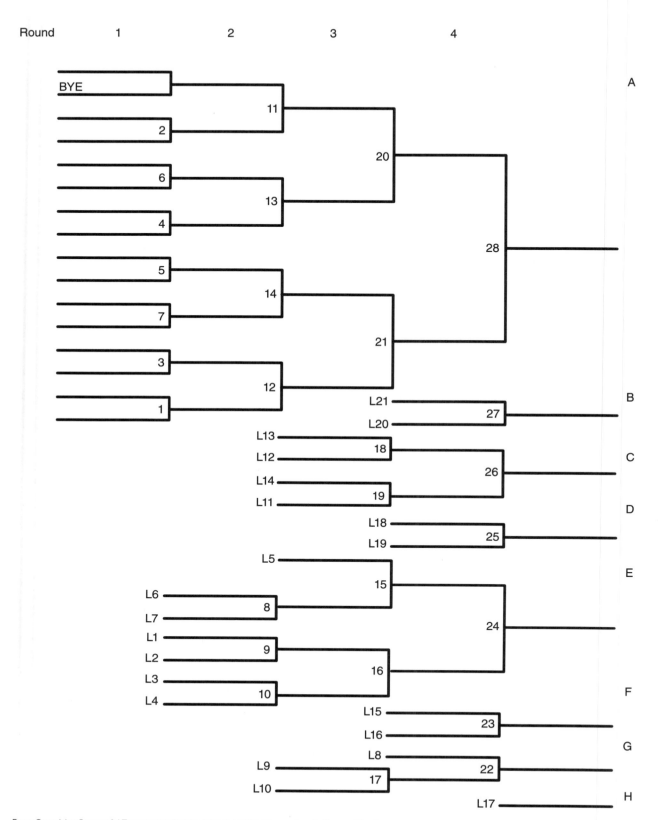

Multilevel tournament with 16 entries

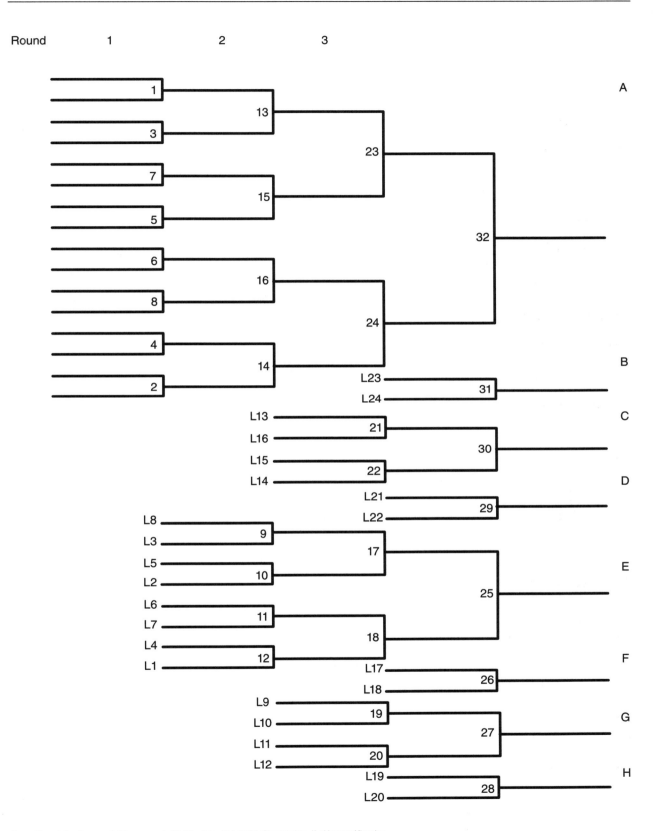

Playing Schedules

FOUR ENTRIES

Two Locations

L I	1	4
L II	2	3

FIVE ENTRIES

Two Locations

L I	2	3	6
L II	1	4	5

SIX ENTRIES

Two Locations

L I	1	4	6	7
L II	2	3	5	

SEVEN ENTRIES

Two Locations

L I	2	4	6	8	9
L II	1	3	5	7	

Three Locations

L I	2	6	9
L II	1	5	8
L III	3	4	7

EIGHT ENTRIES

Two Locations

L I	1	3	5	8	10	12
L II	2	4	6	7	9	11

Three Locations

L I	3	7	8	11	12
L II	1	5	6	10	
L III	2	4		9	

Four Locations

L I	3	8	12
L II	1	7	11
L III	2	5	10
L IV	4	6	9

NINE ENTRIES

Two Locations

L I	1	4	7	9	8	10	14
L II	2	3	5	6	11	12	13

Playing Schedules

Three Locations

L I	1	4	9	10	14
L II	2	7	8	12	13
L III	3	5	6	11	

Four Locations

L I	4	7	9	14
L II	1	6	10	13
L III	2	8	12	
L IV	3	5	11	

---

10 ENTRIES

Two Locations

L I	1	3	5	7	10	12	14	15
L II	2	4	6	8	9	11	13	

Three Locations

L I	1	5	9	10	15
L II	2	4	7	12	14
L III	3	6	8	11	13

Four Locations

L I	5	7	10	15
L II	1	8	9	14
L III	2	4	12	13
L IV	3	6	11	

---

11 ENTRIES

Two Locations

L I	3	2	6	7	9	12	13	16	17
L II	1	4	5	8	10	11	14	15	

Three Locations

L I	3	4	7	12	13	17
L II	1	6	9	11	15	16
L III	2	8	5	10	14	

Four Locations

L I	7	4	12	16	17
L II	3	5	11	13	
L III	1	6	9	15	
L IV	2	8	10	14	

Five Locations

L I	7	4	12	17
L II	3	5	11	16
L III	1	6	9	13
L IV	2	8	10	15
L V			14	

Playing Schedules

12 ENTRIES

Two Locations

L I	1	4	5	7	9	11	14	16	18	20
L II	2	3	6	8	10	12	13	15	17	19

Three Locations

L I	3	4	5	9	14	16	20
L II	1	7	8	11	13	18	19
L III	2	6	10	12	15	17	

Four Locations

L I	4	5	9	14	20
L II	3	6	11	13	19
L III	1	7	12	16	18
L IV	2	8	10	15	17

13 ENTRIES

Two Locations

L I	1	3	5	7	10	14	13	16	18	20	22
L II	2	4	6	8	9	11	12	15	17	19	21

Three Locations

L I	3	5	6	10	15	16	21	22
L II	1	7	8	12	14	18	20
L III	2	4	9	11	13	17	19

Four Locations

L I	3	5	10	16	18	22
L II	4	6	12	15	20	21
L III	1	7	9	14	19	
L IV	2	8	11	13	17	

Five Locations

L I	5	10	16	15	22
L II	3	7	14	18	21
L III	4	6	13	20	
L IV	1	9	12	19	
L V	2	11	8	17	

Six Locations

L I	1	10	16	22
L II	2	7	15	21
L III	3	6	14	18
L IV	4	8	13	20
L V	5	9	12	19
L VI		11		17

Playing Schedules

14 ENTRIES

Two Locations

L I	1	4	6	8	9	12	14	16	18	19	22	24	25
L II	2	3	5	7	10	11	13	15	17	20	21	23	

Three Locations

L I	3	6	8	12	14	17	19	24	25
L II	1	4	7	10	15	18	21	23	
L III	2	5	9	11	13	16	20	22	

Four Locations

L I	4	6	12	14	19	24	25
L II	3	8	9	10	18	23	
L III	1	7	11	16	20	22	
L IV	2	5	13	15	17	21	

Five Locations

L I	4	6	12	18	19	25
L II	3	8	9	17	23	24
L III	5	7	13	16	22	
L IV	1	10		15	21	
L V	2	11		14	20	

Six Locations (Same as Five Locations)

Seven Locations

L I	6	12	19	25
L II	4	9	14	24
L III	3	8	18	23
L IV	5	7	17	22
L V	1	10	16	21
L VI	2	11	15	20
L VII		13		

15 ENTRIES

Two Locations

L I	1	4	5	7	10	11	13	15	18	20	21	24	26	28
L II	2	3	6	9	8	12	14	16	17	19	22	23	25	27

Three Locations

L I	1	5	7	10	13	18	21	24	27	28
L II	2	4	8	11	15	16	20	23	26	
L III	3	6	9	12	14	17	19	22	25	

Four Locations

L I	1	7	8	13	20	21	28
L II	6	9	10	15	18	24	27
L III	2	5	11	16	19	23	26
L IV	3	4	12	14	17	22	25

Playing Schedules

Five Locations

L I	1	7	13	20	21	28
L II	5	9	16	18	25	27
L III	4	10	12	19	24	26
L IV	2	11	14	15	23	
L V	3	6	8	17	22	

Six Locations

L I	1	13	18	21	28
L II	5	7	16	20	27
L III	4	9	17	19	26
L IV	6	10	8	15	25
L V	2	11	14	22	24
L VI	3	12			23

Seven Locations

L I	7	13	21	28
L II	1	11	20	27
L III	5	12	18	26
L IV	4	14	19	25
L V	6	8	15	24
L VI	2	9	16	23
L VII	3	10	17	22

---

16 ENTRIES

Two Locations

L I	1	3	6	8	9	10	13	15	17	19	21	24	25	27	30	32
L II	2	4	5	7	12	11	14	16	18	20	22	23	26	28	29	31

Three Locations

L I	1	6	8	10	15	17	21	24	26	30	32
L II	2	5	9	11	13	18	19	23	27	29	31
L III	3	4	7	12	14	16	20	22	28	25	

Four Locations

L I	1	8	9	15	17	24	25	32
L II	2	6	12	13	18	23	26	31
L III	3	5	10	14	19	21	27	30
L IV	4	7	11	16	20	22	28	29

Five Locations

L I	1	8	15	17	24	29	32
L II	2	10	13	18	23	30	31
L III	3	12	11	19	21	25	
L IV	5	6	9	20	22	26	
L V	4	7	14	16	28	27	

Playing Schedules

Six Locations

L I	1	8	15	24	29	32
L II	2	9	17	23	30	31
L III	6	12	18	21	25	
L IV	5	10	13	22	26	
L V	3	11	14	19	27	
L VI	4	7	16	20	28	

Seven Locations

L I	1	15	18	24	26	32
L II	2	8	9	23	27	31
L III	6	10	20	21	28	30
L IV	5	11	16	22		29
L V	7	13	17	19		25
L VI	3	14				27
L VII	4	12				28

Eight Locations

L I	8	15	24	32
L II	1	10	23	31
L III	2	11	21	30
L IV	6	13	22	29
L V	5	14	17	25
L VI	7	16	18	26
L VII	3	9	19	27
L VIII	4	12	20	28

CHAPTER 4

Double-Elimination Tournaments

The top level of the double-elimination tournament is much the same as that of a single-elimination tournament, with only the final game being slightly different, as I will explain soon. Seeding is the same as for single elimination, but use only the advantage seeding chart, which we provide for tournaments with 16 or fewer entries (page 24). Place the name of each player (or team) who wins on the draw sheet to the right of that player's or team's previously recorded game. In a double-elimination format, the first time an entry loses a game (or match), the entry simply moves down to the appropriate position on the losers' bracket. Those who lose in the losers' bracket are eliminated (see figure 4.1, page 70). The ultimate winner of the losers' bracket has lost one game and can be eliminated only after losing twice. Thus, this winner moves up to play the winner of the winners' bracket. If the winner of the losers' bracket wins this game or match, the same two opponents must play one more game because the winner of the winners' bracket has lost only once. This type of tournament requires many rounds because for every round played on the winners' bracket, two are played in the losers' bracket.

To prevent players from playing each other twice in close succession, losers of a bracket cross over to the next major bracket. We have built this into the schedules, illustrated in figures 4.2, 4.3, and 4.4 (pages 71 and 72). However, there are three times when playing the same entry twice cannot be avoided. With correct seeding, the first- and second-seeded players will play each other twice; in fact, if these two entries split their games, they will play each other three times. The second situation in which two entries would play each other twice is when there are only three entries. Also, it is possible that lower-seeded players who defeat higher-seeded players in an early round will play their opponents twice.

The procedure for large double-elimination tournaments is the same as for small ones. To conserve space, we have not prepared separate draw sheets for large numbers of entries. However, you can organize a tournament of this size easily in little additional time. If you have more than 16 entries—for example, 32—it would be best to seed them into four double-elimination draw sheets of 8 entries each. The winners of those draws would be placed in a predetermined manner on a final draw sheet of 4 entries. If you had 64 entries, you might select four draw sheets of 16 entries or eight draw sheets of 8 entries, with winners going to a final draw sheet of either 4 or 8 entries, respectively. For other options in managing a large number of entries, see chapter 7.

If you wish to know how many games or matches your double-elimination tournament will require, the formula is as follows:

$$(\text{Number of entries} - 1) \times 2 = \text{number of games}$$

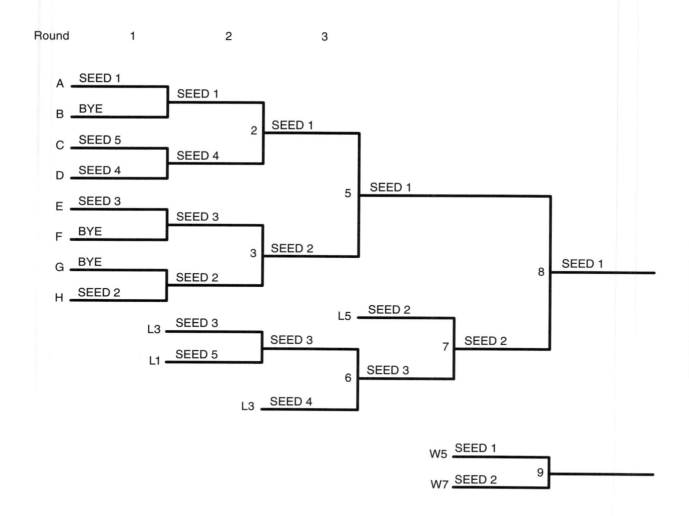

Figure 4.1　Double elimination with five entries.

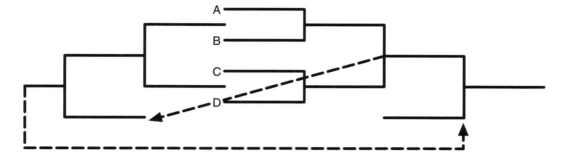

Figure 4.2   Double elimination with four or fewer entries.

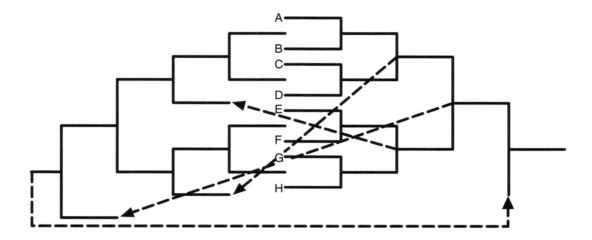

Figure 4.3   Double elimination with five to eight entries.

Advantages of a Double-Elimination Tournament

- Each entrant is guaranteed two games.
- An entrant who loses once can still win the championship.
- Seeding is not crucial.
- Few locations are required.
- A better measure of players' or teams' ability is provided compared to a single-elimination format.

Disadvantages of a Double-Elimination Tournament

- Some players may play many games; others play few.
- Many rounds are required.
- Use of multiple locations is not maximized.

The double-elimination format is best used when playing areas are limited and final standings are important.

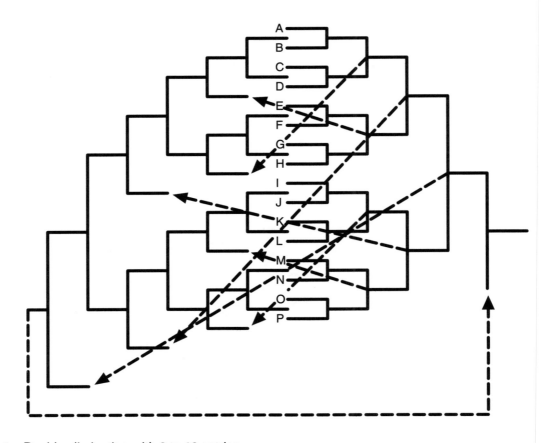

Figure 4.4 Double elimination with 9 to 16 entries.

Using the Software

1. Open the Double Elimination folder.
2. Select your number of entries and locations. For example, DE 5E 2L is double elimination, 5 entries, 2 locations (see figure 4.5).
3. Fill in the competition name, competition date, seeds, locations, dates, and times, using the "tab" button to move from field to field. *Note:* If you fail to push the tab button, the field will not be entered.
4. Save the file to your hard drive.
5. Print a copy.

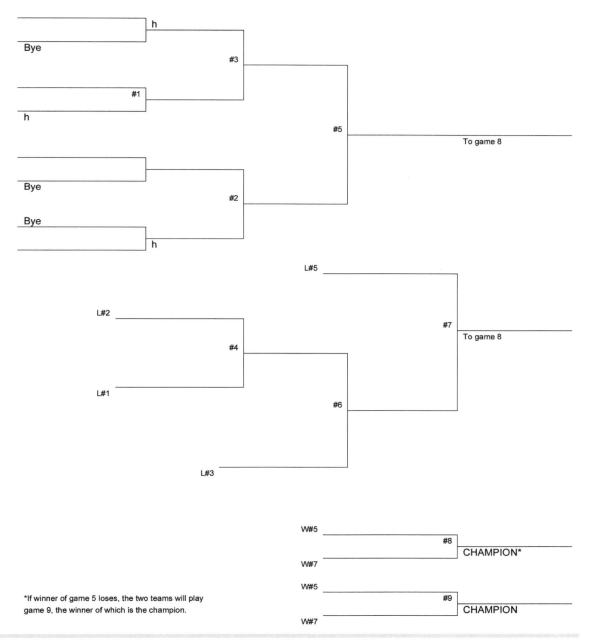

Figure 4.5 Sample double-elimination bracket for five entries, two locations.

Double-elimination tournament with 3 entries

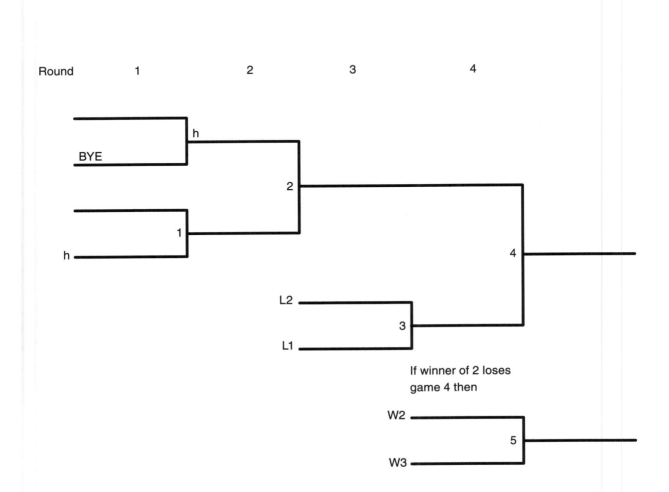

Round   1   2   3   4

If winner of 2 loses game 4 then

From *Organizing Successful Tournaments* (3e) by John Byl, 2006, Champaign, IL: Human Kinetics.

Double-elimination tournament with 4 entries

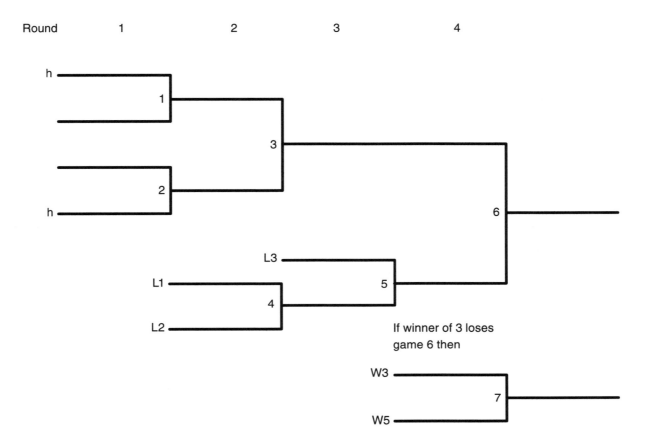

Round   1   2   3   4

If winner of 3 loses game 6 then

From *Organizing Successful Tournaments* (3e) by John Byl, 2006, Champaign, IL: Human Kinetics.

Double-elimination tournament with 5 entries

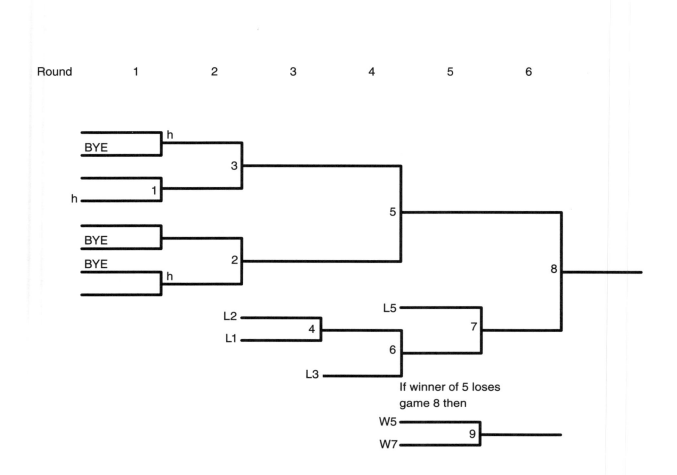

Round   1   2   3   4   5   6

If winner of 5 loses
game 8 then

From *Organizing Successful Tournaments* (3e) by John Byl, 2006, Champaign, IL: Human Kinetics.

Double-elimination tournament with 6 entries

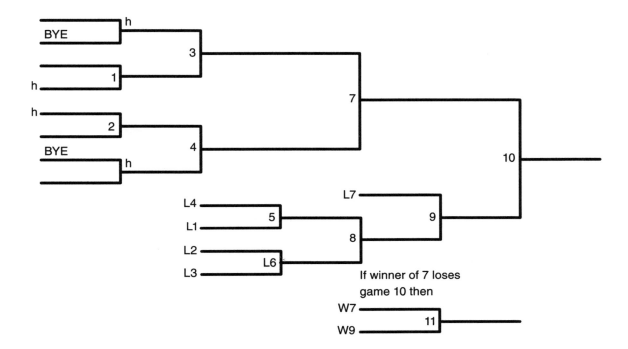

From *Organizing Successful Tournaments* (3e) by John Byl, 2006, Champaign, IL: Human Kinetics.

77

Double-elimination tournament with 7 entries

Round 1   2   3   4   5   6

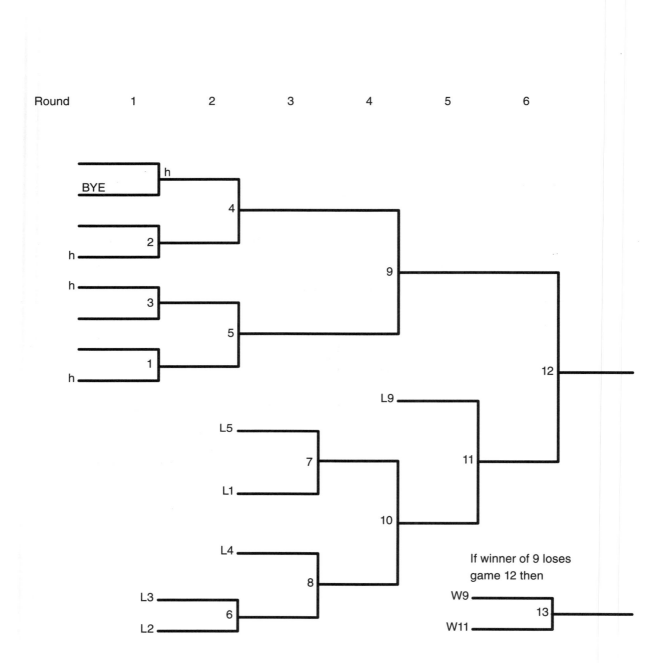

From *Organizing Successful Tournaments* (3e) by John Byl, 2006, Champaign, IL: Human Kinetics.

Double-elimination tournament with 8 entries

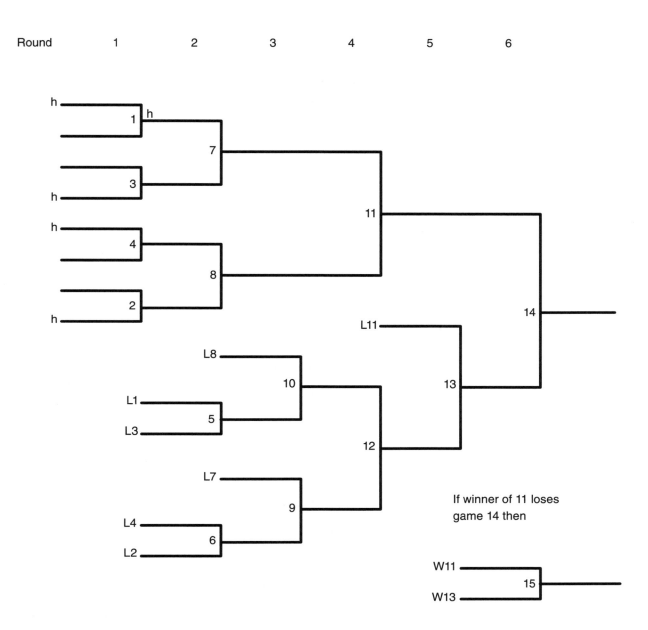

Round   1   2   3   4   5   6

If winner of 11 loses
game 14 then

From *Organizing Successful Tournaments* (3e) by John Byl, 2006, Champaign, IL: Human Kinetics.

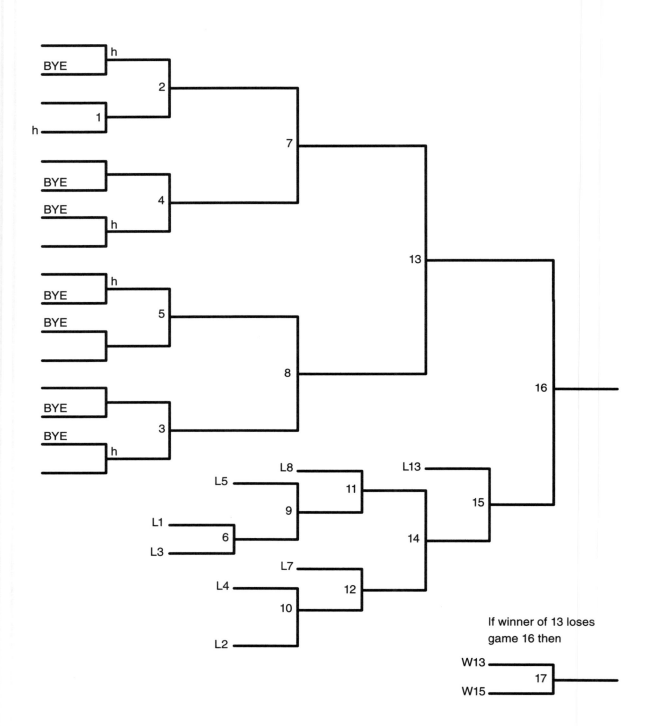

If winner of 13 loses
game 16 then

From *Organizing Successful Tournaments* (3e) by John Byl, 2006, Champaign, IL: Human Kinetics.

Double-elimination tournament with 10 entries

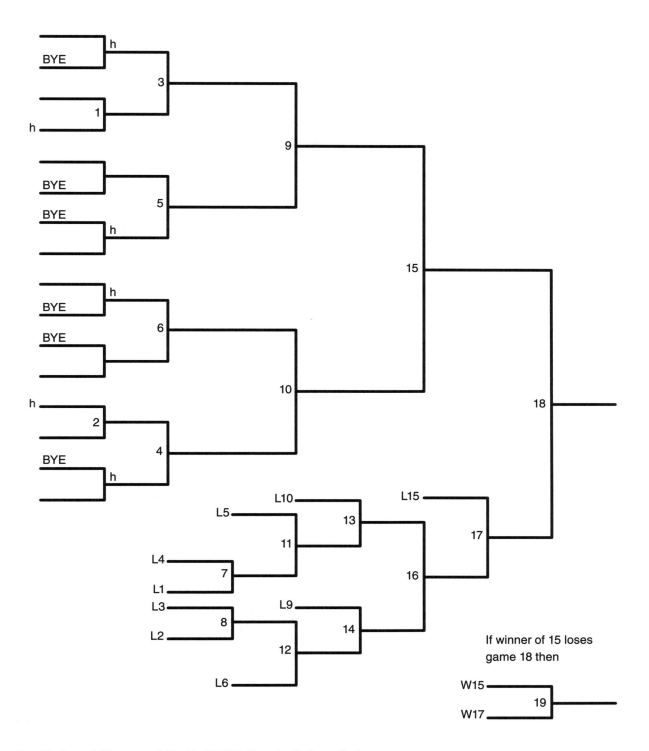

Round   1   2   3   4   5   6   7   8

If winner of 15 loses game 18 then

From *Organizing Successful Tournaments* (3e) by John Byl, 2006, Champaign, IL: Human Kinetics.

Double-elimination tournament with 11 entries

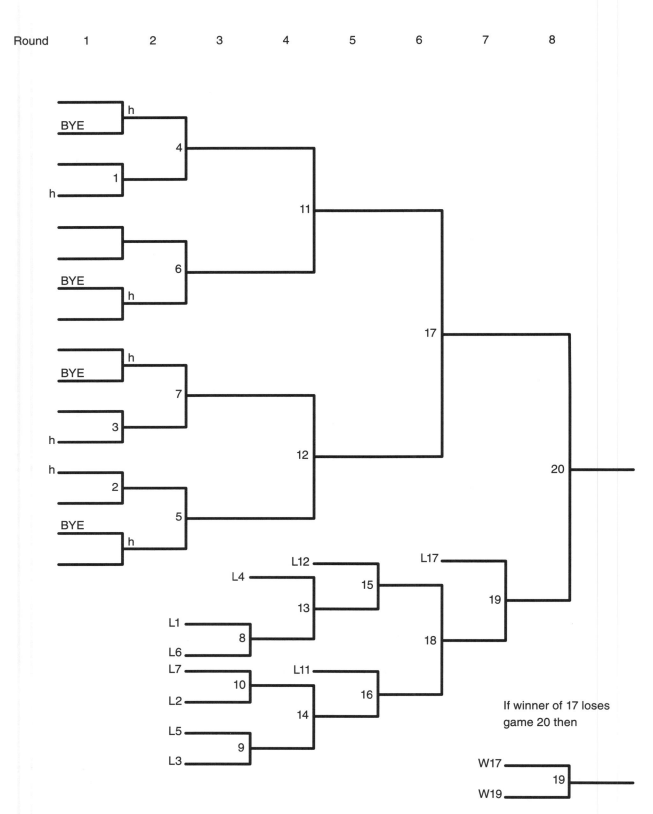

Round   1   2   3   4   5   6   7   8

If winner of 17 loses
game 20 then

W17
W19
19

From *Organizing Successful Tournaments* (3e) by John Byl, 2006, Champaign, IL: Human Kinetics.

Double-elimination tournament with 12 entries

Round   1   2   3   4   5   6   7   8

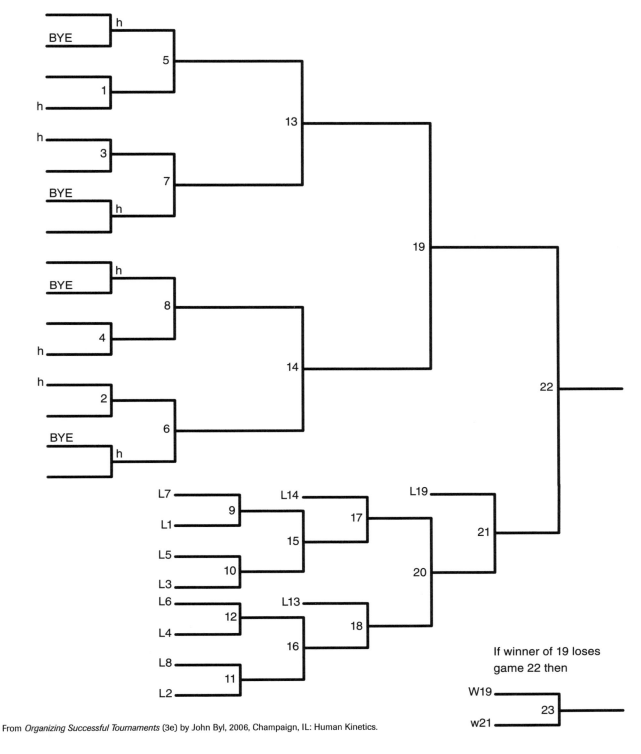

If winner of 19 loses game 22 then

Double-elimination tournament with 13 entries

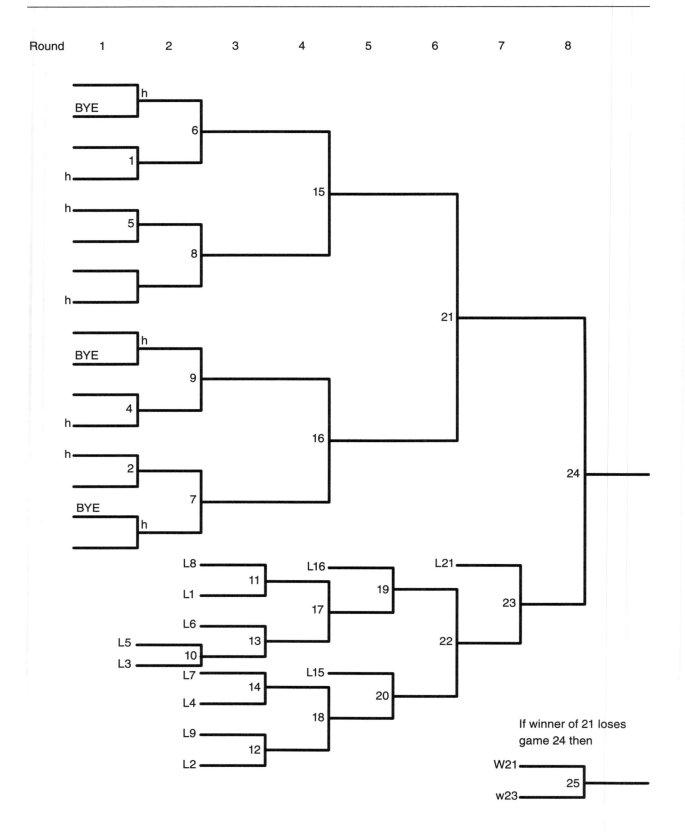

Round 1 2 3 4 5 6 7 8

If winner of 21 loses game 24 then

From *Organizing Successful Tournaments* (3e) by John Byl, 2006, Champaign, IL: Human Kinetics.

Double-elimination tournament with 14 entries

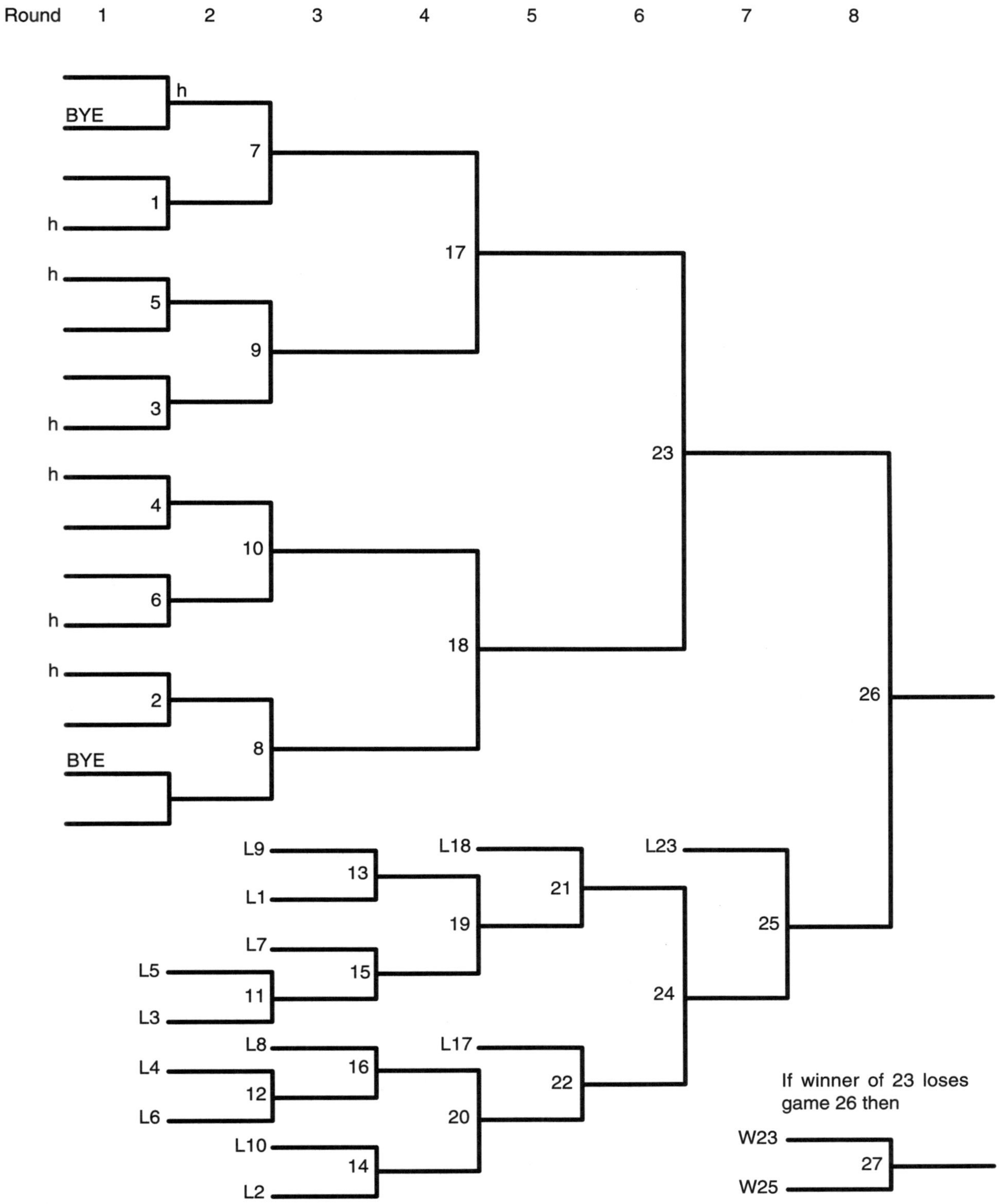

Round   1   2   3   4   5   6   7   8

BYE — h
h — 1
7

h — 5
h — 3
9

17

h — 4
h — 6
10

18

h — 2
BYE
8

23

26

L9
L1
13

L18
21

L7
L5
L3
11
15

19

L23
25

L8
L4
L6
12
16

L17
22

L10
L2
14

20

24

If winner of 23 loses game 26 then

W23
W25
27

From Organizing Successful Tournaments (3e) by John Byl, 2006, Champaign, IL: Human Kinetics.

85

Double-elimination tournament with 15 entries

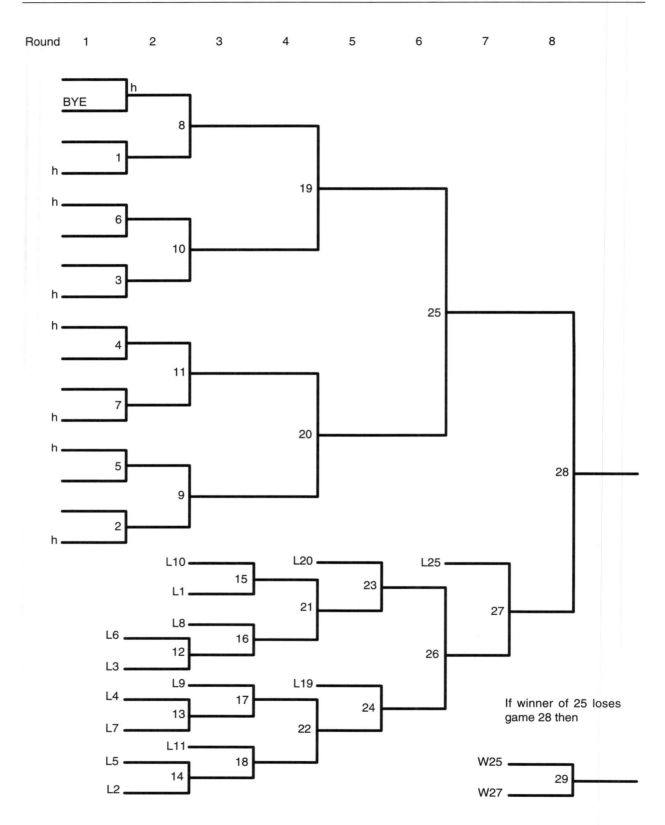

From Organizing Successful Tournaments (3e) by John Byl, 2006, Champaign, IL: Human Kinetics.

Double-elimination tournament with 16 entries

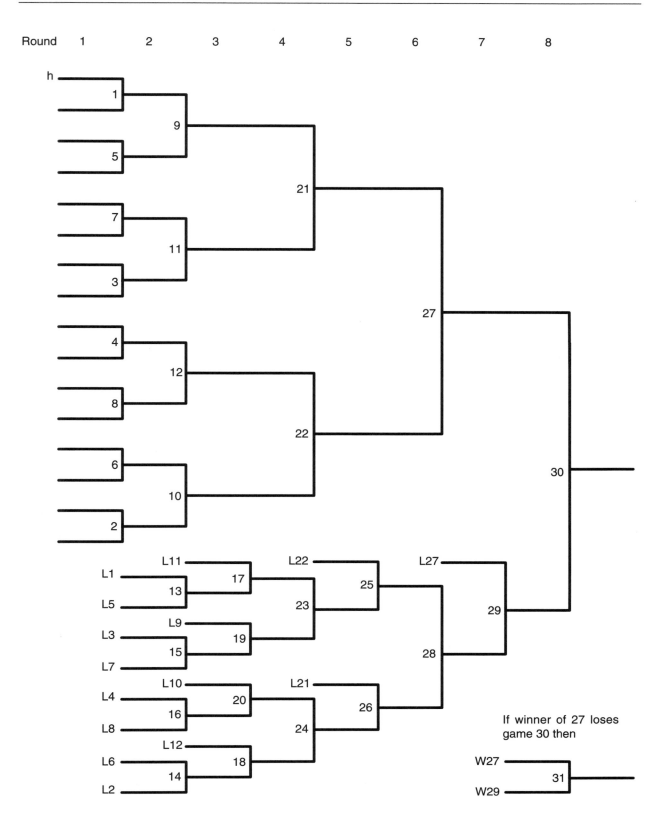

From Organizing Successful Tournaments (3e) by John Byl, 2006, Champaign, IL: Human Kinetics.

Playing Schedules

FOUR ENTRIES

Two Locations

L I	2	3	5	6	(7)
L II	1	4			

FIVE ENTRIES

Two Locations

L I	1	3	5	7	8	(9)
L II	2	4	6			

SIX ENTRIES

Two Locations

L I	1	4	5	7	9	10	(11)
L II	2	3	6	8		

SEVEN ENTRIES

Two Locations

L I	2	4	5	7	9	11	12 (13)
L II	1	3	6	8	10		

Three Locations

L I	2	5	7	9	11	12 (13)
L II	3	6	8	10		
L III	1	4				

EIGHT ENTRIES

Two Locations

L I	2	3	6	8	10	11	13	14 (15)
L II	1	4	5	7	9	12		

Three Locations

L I	3	7	8	10	11	13	14 (15)
L II	2	4	6	9	12		
L III	1	5					

Four Locations

L I	3	8	10	11	13	14 (15)
L II	4	6	9	12		
L III	2	7				
L IV	1	5				

NINE ENTRIES

Two Locations

L I	1	4	6	8	10	11	13	15	16 (17)
L II	3	2	5	7	9	12	14		

Playing Schedules

Three Locations

L I	4	5	8	10	11	13	15	16 (17)
L II	1	6	7	9	12	14		
L III	3	2						

Four Locations

L I	4	6	8	11	13	15	16 (17)
L II	1	2	10	12	14		
L III	5		7				
L IV	3		9				

10 ENTRIES

Two Locations

L I	1	4	5	7	10	11	13	15	17	18 (19)
L II	2	3	6	8	9	12	14	16		

Three Locations

L I	5	6	7	10	13	15	17	18 (19)
L II	1	4	8	11	14	16		
L III	2	3	9	12				

Four Locations

L I	1	5	7	10	13	15	17	18 (19)
L II	2	6	8	11	14	16		
L III		4		9				
L IV		3		12				

11 ENTRIES

Two Locations

L I	1	3	6	7	10	12	14	15	17	19	20 (21)
L II	2	4	5	8	9	11	13	16	18		

Three Locations

L I	1	6	7	12	14	15	17	19	20 (21)
L II	2	5	8	11	13	16	18		
L III	3	4	9	10					

Four Locations

L I	1	6	8	12	15	17	19 (21)
L II	2	7	9	14	16	18	
L III	3	5	10	11			
L IV		4		13			

12 ENTRIES

Two Locations

L I	1	4	6	7	9	11	14	16	17	19	21	22 (23)
L II	2	3	5	8	10	12	13	15	18	20		

Playing Schedules

Three Locations

L I	1	6	7	9	14	16	17	19	21	22 (23)
L II	2	4	8	11	13	15	18	20		
L III	3	5	10	12						

Four Locations

L I	1	7	9	14	17	19	21	22	(23)
L II	2	8	11	16	18	20			
L III	4	6	12	13					
L IV	3	5	10	15					

13 ENTRIES

Two Locations

L I	1	5	4	8	10	11	12	16	18	19	21	23	24 (25)
L II	2	3	6	7	9	13	14	15	17	20	22		

Three Locations

L I	1	6	8	10	15	16	19	21	23	24 (25)
L II	2	4	9	11	14	18	20	22		
L III	3	5	7	12	13	17				

Four Locations

L I	1	8	10	16	18	19	21	23	24 (25)
L II	2	4	9	15	17	20	22		
L III	3	7	11	14					
L IV	5	6	12	13					

Five Locations

L I	1	8	11	16	19	21	23	24 (25)	
L II	2	10	12	18	20	22			
L III	4	9	14	15					
L IV	5	7	13	17					
L V	3	6							

14 ENTRIES

Two Locations

L I	1	3	6	8	9	11	13	16	18	20	21	23	25	26 (27)
L II	2	4	5	7	10	12	15	14	17	19	22	24		

Three Locations

L I	1	6	9	11	13	18	20	21	23	25	26 (27)
L II	2	5	8	10	14	17	19	22	24		
L III	3	4	7	12	15	16					

Four Locations

L I	1	6	9	13	18	21	23	25	26 (27)
L II	2	5	11	14	20	22	24		
L III	3	8	10	16	17				
L IV	4	7	12	15	19				

Playing Schedules

Five Locations (Same as Four Locations)

Six Locations

L I	1	9	13	18	21	23	25	26 (27)
L II	2	11	14	20	22	24		
L III	6	10	16	17				
L IV	5	12	15	19				
L V	3	8						
L VI	4	7						

15 ENTRIES

Two Locations

L I	1	6	7	5	12	10	14	15	18	20	22	23	25	27	28 (29)
L II	2	3	4	8	9	11	13	16	17	19	21	24	26		

Three Locations

L I	1	7	10	12	13	18	20	22	23	25	27	28 (29)
L II	4	6	5	11	15	17	19	21	24	26		
L III	2	3	8	9	14	16						

Four Locations

L I	1	5	10	13	20	22	23	25	27	28 (29)
L II	3	7	12	15	19	21	24	26		
L III	4	6	11	16	17					
L IV	2	8	9	14	18					

Five Locations

L I	1	10	12	15	20	23	25	27	28 (29)
L II	5	9	13	18	22	24	26		
L III	6	7	11	17	19				
L IV	3	8	14	16	21				
L V	2	4							

Six Locations (Same as Five Locations)

Seven Locations

L I	1	10	15	20	23	25	27	28 (29)
L II	5	12	18	22	24	26		
L III	7	11	17	19				
L IV	6	13	16	21				
L V	3	9						
L VI	4	14						
L VII	2	8						

16 ENTRIES

Two Locations

L I	2	3	5	8	10	11	14	15	17	20	22	24	25	27	29	30	(31)
L II	1	4	6	7	9	12	13	16	18	19	21	23	26	28			

Playing Schedules

Three Locations

L I	5	6	8	11	15	16	21	22	25	27	29	30 (31)
L II	2	7	9	12	14	17	20	24	26	28		
L III	1	3	4	10	13	18	19	23				

Four Locations

L I	5	8	11	15	17	22	25	27	29	30 (31)
L II	6	7	12	16	18	24	26	28		
L III	2	3	10	14	20	21				
L IV	1	4	9	13	19	23				

Five Locations (Same as Four Locations)

Six Locations

L I	5	10	11	17	22	25	27	29	30 (31)
L II	6	8	15	18	24	26	28		
L III	2	9	12	20	21				
L IV	1	7	16	19	23				
L V		3	14						
L VI		4	13						

Seven Locations (Same as Six Locations)

Eight Locations

L I	5	11	17	22	25	27	29	30 (31)
L II	6	15	18	24	26	28		
L III	8	12	20	21				
L IV	7	16	19	23				
L V	3	10						
L VI	4	14						
L VII	2	9						
L VIII	1	13						

C H A P T E R 5

Round Robin Tournaments and Leagues

Round robin play involves each entry playing all other entries. Round robin tournaments with many entries take a long time to complete. If you wish to use this tournament with a large number of entries, the best strategy is to divide the entries into two, three, or more divisions. In this chapter we explain the round robin tournament, including variations for divisional play, and include necessary schedules and support materials.

Although much of the following discussion deals with a one- or two-day tournament, a round robin format could also form the schedule for an entire season of play for any league. All the schedules identify home and away teams. This identification is helpful not only for league formats but also in tournaments involving sports such as baseball in which the home team bats second or hockey where the home team is the last team to be permitted to make a line change.

Seeding is unimportant to the final outcome in a round robin; however, the tournament might be more interesting if the deciding games are at the end—so that in the final game seed 1 plays seed 2, seed 3 plays seed 4, 5 plays 6, and so on. Typically, the higher seeds compete on the best location in the final round. For example, if there were six teams and three courts, seeds 1 and 2 compete on location 1, seeds 3 and 4 on location 2, and seeds 5 and 6 on location 3. Record sheets are provided at the end of the chapter for up to 10 entries; the CD includes a recording sheet for each of the schedules. We have prepared the playing schedules to make your work easier and more precise.

Beyond having the deciding games be the finals, two other principles influenced the organization of the playing schedules.

1. Minimize the number of games any team plays in a row. Although it is often unavoidable that teams play several games in a row, we have made every attempt to equalize this possibility among all teams.

2. Equalize the number of games each entry plays on each location. (If one location in the tournament is the most or least desirable, it would hardly be fair for any entry to be advantaged or disadvantaged by playing a high percentage of its games on that location.)

This second principle has further detailed applications. Sometimes, for example, with six entries, each entry plays five games (or matches). If there are two locations on which to compete, the top seeds are assigned three games on location 1 and the bottom seeds assigned three games on location 2.

The second principle also applies to divisional competitions. If divisions are assigned different locations, then the division with the number 1 seed was assigned location 1, the division with the number 2 seed was assigned location 2, and so on. If there are two divisions and three locations, every effort has been made to have division 1 compete on location 1, division 2 on location 2, and division 1 and 2 share location 3 as equally as possible.

Home and away schedules use a similar logic. Using the example of a six-entry schedule, there are five games to be played. In such cases, the higher seeds play three home games and the lower seeds play two home games. Furthermore, when two seeds are competing that are next to each other in ranking, for example, 1 and 2 or 14 and 15, then the home game would go to the higher seed (keep in mind that the *higher* seed is the *lower* number; that is, a 1 seed is higher than a 2 seed). When a schedule is repeated two times, the home and away schedule would alternate; if player or team 4 played at the home of 7 the first time, then 7 would compete at the home of 4 the next time. For seeds that are next to each other in ranking, the first game would be at the home of the lower ranked seed and the second game would be at the home of the higher ranked seed.

Every effort was made to consistently apply these principles. However, most schedules did not work out perfectly, so various principles were weighted against each other as each schedule was crafted.

You might need to build in a rest period, especially when using many locations. You can facilitate this rest period as a rule stating that all entries may have a minimum of so many minutes rest between games or matches. Or, you may wish to establish longer breaks at certain points in the tournament, perhaps following every fourth game or match.

Because all entries play each other, the final ranking is determined by the cumulative outcome of all games. Usually 2 points are awarded for a win, 1 point for a tie, 0 points for a loss, –1 for a default (if a team or player gives advance notice that they cannot compete), and –2 for a no-show (if a team or player gives no notice or inadequate advance notice that they can't compete). Should there be a tie in the standings, you may turn to chapter 9, which describes various tiebreaking procedures for tournaments.

Should you decide to make your own schedule, take the following into account.

1.   Use rotations to ensure that all entries play each other. The schedules presented in this chapter use the following rotations:

If there is an even number, A stays while the others rotate clockwise (figure 5.1).

Figure 5.1   Even-number rotation.

If there is an odd number, X stays while the others rotate clockwise (figure 5.2)

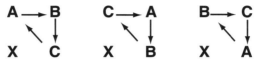

Figure 5.2   Odd-number rotation.

This rotation ensures that all entries play each other, but it leaves uneven schedules. For example, one team or player might play four games in a row, have three breaks, then play another four, while another team or player might have two games, one break, two games, one break, two games, one break, and two games. The latter has a far superior schedule. To balance this as much as possible, we rearranged the schedules in this manual and on the CD.

2.   The locations of some tournaments may vary in quality. To balance this, the entries are further rearranged. If more than 16 entries participate, the tournament will likely become excessively long. Sixteen entries require 120 games. It is unlikely that you would wish to exceed this number and still use the round robin approach. Instead, you would be better off to split the group into two, three, or four divisions and use one of the approaches suggested in the following sections.

Here is the formula for determining the number of games in a round robin tournament:

[Number of entries × (number of entries – 1)] / 2

Round Robin Double Split

The round robin double split is simply a round robin tournament with entries split into two divisions. The principles and procedures are the same as for the round robin, but there are some differences that we should note.

There are two divisions, and each needs its own recording sheet. The seeding is also different; at the end of division play, the top players from one division play the top players from the other division to determine overall tournament ranking. As in single elimination, the top-ranked player goes in the first division, the second in the second division, the third in the first division, and so on.

If this were not done, major problems might develop. For example, if we had eight entries and placed the top four in division 1 and the bottom four in division 2, the third- and fourth-ranked entries would not make it to the finals. At best, the fifth- and sixth-ranked entries would make it to the finals. Obviously, this is undesirable.

In division play it is often advantageous, for scheduling and player interest, to play as many as possible of the intradivisional games at the same locations (identified as "Location Different" [LD] on the CD). If you prefer, you can also have the divisions share all locations equally (identified as "Location Shared" [LS] on the CD). If many locations are available, assign each division several locations and evenly distribute entries.

To determine the number of games required, calculate the number of games per division, using the round robin formula (page 95), then add the number of games required for the appropriate playoff format:

Division 1 + division 2 + playoffs = number of games

Round Robin Triple Split

The round robin triple split is a round robin tournament in which the entries split into three divisions. The principles and procedures for placing the entries into divisions are basically the same as for the round robin double split, but entries are now divided into three divisions. As with any round robin, you could use this format for a one- or two-day tournament or as the structure for league play involving three divisions.

To determine the number of games required, calculate the number of games per division using the round robin formula (page 95), then add the number of games required for the chosen playoff format:

Division 1 + division 2 + division 3 + playoffs = number of games

Round Robin Quadruple Split

The round robin quadruple split is a round robin tournament with the entries split into four divisions. The principles and procedures for placing the entries into divisions are basically the same as for the other round robin split tournaments, but entries are now divided into four divisions.

To determine the number of games required, calculate the number of games per division, using the round robin formula (page 95), then add the number of games required for the chosen playoff format:

Division 1 + division 2 + division 3 + division 4 + playoffs = number of games

Seeding for Divisions and Playoffs

When there are two or more divisions place the highest seed in division 1, the next in division 2, the next in division 3, and so on. If, for example we have nine entries to divide into three divisions, division 1 will consist of seeds 1, 4, and 7; division 2 will consist of seeds 2, 5, and 8; and division 3 will consist of seeds 3, 6, and 9. If we had 10 entries for three divisions, seed 10 is added to division 3. If we had 11 entries for three divisions, seed 10 is added to division 2, and seed 11 is added to division 3. The division with the highest seed is always in the smaller division, the one requiring one fewer games per entry.

Because seedings can be inaccurate, it is always important to bring to the play-offs the number of entries you seek to rank. If you want to know who the top two teams are, you must carry over the top two teams from each division. If you want to know who the top three teams are, carry over the top three teams from each division. When positioning these entries onto a single-elimination playoff bracket, it is also important to keep entries from the same divisions as far apart as possible on the playoff bracket. For example, if you have four divisions, and you want to know who the top four teams are, it should be possible that if the top four teams were unfortunately placed all in the same division that they all make it to the playoffs. These playoff schedules are provided on the CD under Round Robin Playoffs.

Select the appropriate single-elimination bracket and position the entries as indicated on table 5.1. Tables 5.2-5.5 show the seeding for various number of divisions and entries.

Table 5.1   Seeding Chart for Playoffs by Number of Divisions and Finishers Sought

Two divisions			Three divisions			Four divisions			Five divisions			Six divisions	
Top 1	Top 2	Top 3-4	Top 1	Top 2	Top 3-4	Top 1	Top 2	Top 3-4	Top 1	Top 2	Top 3	Top 1	Top 2
1/1	1/1	1/1	1/1	1/1	1/1	1/1	1/1	1/1	1/1	1/1	1/1	1/1	1/1
1/2	2/2	4/2	Bye	Bye	Bye	1/4	2/3	4/4	Bye	Bye	Bye	Bye	Bye
	2/1	3/1	1/3	2/3	3/3	1/3	2/2	3/2	1/5	2/5	2/5	1/5	2/3
	1/2	2/2	1/2	2/2	3/2	1/2	1/4	2/3	1/4	2/2	2/2	1/4	2/2
		2/1		1/3	2/2		1/3	2/2	1/3	1/5	1/5	1/3	1/5
		3/2		2/1	4/1		2/1	3/3	Bye	Bye	3/1	1/6	2/6
		4/1		Bye	Bye		2/4	4/1	Bye	Bye	3/3	Bye	Bye
		1/2		1/2	1/3		1/2	1/4	1/2	1/4	1/4	1/2	1/4
					2/1			1/3		1/3	1/3		1/3
					Bye			4/2		Bye	3/4		Bye
					4/2			3/4		Bye	3/2		2/5
					2/3			2/1		2/1	2/1		1/6
					3/1			2/4		2/3	2/3		2/1
					4/3			3/1		2/4	2/4		2/4
					Bye			4/3		Bye	3/5		Bye
					1/2			1/2		1/2	1/2		1/2

Legend: 1/1 means number 1 finisher of division 1; 2/1 means number 2 finisher of division 1.

Table 5.2 Seeding for Two Divisions—6 to 16 Entries

	6	7	8	9	10	11	12	13	14	15	16
Division 1	1	1	1	1	1	1	1	1	1	1	1
	3	3	3	3	3	3	3	3	3	3	3
	5	5	5	5	5	5	5	5	5	5	5
			7	7	7	7	7	7	7	7	7
					9	9	9	9	9	9	9
							11	11	11	11	11
									13	13	13
											15
Division 2	2	2	2	2	2	2	2	2	2	2	2
	4	4	4	4	4	4	4	4	4	4	4
	6	6	6	6	6	6	6	6	6	6	6
		7	8	8	8	8	8	8	8	8	8
				9	10	10	10	10	10	10	10
						11	12	12	12	12	12
								13	14	14	14
										15	16

Table 5.3 Seeding for Three Divisions—9 to 16 Entries

	9	10	11	12	13	14	15	16
Division 1	1	1	1	1	1	1	1	1
	4	4	4	4	4	4	4	4
	7	7	7	7	7	7	7	7
				10	10	10	10	10
							13	13
Division 2	2	2	2	2	2	2	2	2
	5	5	5	5	5	5	5	5
	8	8	8	8	8	8	8	8
			10	11	11	11	11	11
						13	14	14
Division 3	3	3	3	3	3	3	3	3
	6	6	6	6	6	6	6	6
	9	9	9	9	9	9	9	9
		10	11	12	12	12	12	12
					13	14	15	15
								16

Table 5.4 Seeding for Four Divisions—12 to 16 Entries

	12	13	14	15	16
Division 1	1	1	1	1	1
	5	5	5	5	5
	9	9	9	9	9
					13
Division 2	2	2	2	2	2
	6	6	6	6	6
	10	10	10	10	10
				13	14
Division 3	3	3	3	3	3
	7	7	7	7	7
	11	11	11	11	11
			13	14	15
Division 4	4	4	4	4	4
	8	8	8	8	8
	12	12	12	12	12
		13	14	15	16

Table 5.5 Seeding for Five Divisions—15 or 16 Entries

	15	16
Division 1	1	1
	6	6
	11	11
Division 2	2	2
	7	7
	12	12
Division 3	3	3
	8	8
	13	13
Division 4	4	4
	9	9
	14	14
Division 5	5	5
	10	10
	15	15
		16

Advantages of a Round Robin Tournament

- All players play each other, so true standings result.
- Seeding is unimportant.
- Multiple locations are used effectively.
- No one is eliminated.

Disadvantages of a Round Robin Tournament

- Many games (or matches) are required.
- Many games might be lopsided.

A round robin format is best used for league play and whenever true standings are essential.

 # Using the Software

1. Open the Round Robin folder by the number of entries (either 3 to 8 entries or 9 to 16 entries).
2. Select your folder by location and number of rotations. You may choose any of the following:
   - Locations Different One Rotation
   - Locations Different Two Rotations
   - Locations Shared One Rotation
   - Locations Shared Two Rotations
3. Select your number of entries and locations. For example, RR 14E 2D 2L is round robin, 14 entries, 2 divisions, 2 locations. Figures 5.3-5.5 show sample result sheets based on the number of entries.
4. Fill in the competition name, competition date, seeds, locations, dates, and times, using the "tab" button to move from field to field. *Note:* If you fail to use the tab button, the field will not be entered.
5. Save the file to your hard drive.
6. Print a copy.

RESULTS

	Entry Name		1			2			3			4		W	T	L	Df	Ns	Pts	Rk
1	Trojans				50	-	48	64	-	22	68	-	62	3	0	0	0	0		1
2	Spartans	48	-	50				66	-	64	57	-	48	2	0	1	0	0		2
3	Lions	22	-	64	64	-	66				45	-	54	0	0	3	0	0		4
4	Chiefs	62	-	68	48	-	57	54	-	45				1	0	2	0	0		3

W=Win, T=Tie, L=Loss, Df=Default
Ns=No-show, Pts=Points, Rk=Rank

Figure 5.3 Sample result sheet—4 entries, 1 division, 1 location, 1 rotation.

RESULTS

	Entry Name	W	T	L	Df	Ns	Pts	Rk
1								
2								
3								
4								
5								
6								
7								

W=Win, T=Tie, L=Loss, Df=Default
Ns=No-show, Pts=Points, Rk=Rank

Figure 5.4 Blank result sheet—7 entries, 1 division, 1 location, 1 rotation.

RESULTS

	Entry Name	W	T	L	Df	Ns	Pts	Rk
1								
2								
3								
4								
5								
6								
7								
8								

W=Win, T=Tie, L=Loss, Df=Default
Ns=No-show, Pts=Points, Rk=Rank

Figure 5.5 Blank result sheet—8 entries, 1 division, 1 locaton, 1 rotation.

Three Entries at One Location

Tournament name _____

Tournament date _____

Tournament location _____

Seed 1	
Seed 2	
Seed 3	

Game	Home	Away	Date	Time	Results
1	3	1			
2	2	3			
1	1	2			

Four Entries at One Location

Tournament name _____

Tournament date _____

Tournament location _____

Seed 1	
Seed 2	
Seed 3	
Seed 4	

Game	Home	Away	Date	Time	Results
1	1	3			
2	2	4			
3	4	1			
4	2	3			
5	3	4			
6	1	2			

From *Organizing Successful Tournaments* (3e) by John Byl, 2006, Champaign, IL: Human Kinetics.

Five Entries at One Location

Tournament name _____

Tournament date _____

Tournament location _____

Seed 1	
Seed 2	
Seed 3	
Seed 4	
Seed 5	

Game	Home	Away	Date	Time	Results
1	4	1			
2	5	3			
3	2	4			
4	3	1			
5	5	2			
6	3	4			
7	1	5			
8	2	3			
9	4	5			
10	1	2			

From *Organizing Successful Tournaments* (3e) by John Byl, 2006, Champaign, IL: Human Kinetics.

Six Entries at One Location

Tournament name _____

Tournament date _____

Tournament location _____

Seed 1	
Seed 2	
Seed 3	
Seed 4	
Seed 5	
Seed 6	

Game	Home	Away	Date	Time	Results
1	3	1			
2	4	6			
3	1	5			
4	2	4			
5	5	3			
6	6	2			
7	1	4			
8	2	5			
9	3	6			
10	4	5			
11	6	1			
12	2	3			
13	5	6			
14	3	4			
15	1	2			

From *Organizing Successful Tournaments* (3e) by John Byl, 2006, Champaign, IL: Human Kinetics.

Seven Entries at One Location

Tournament name _____

Tournament date _____

Tournament location _____

Seed 1	
Seed 2	
Seed 3	
Seed 4	
Seed 5	
Seed 6	
Seed 7	

Game	Home	Away	Date	Time	Results
1	7	5			
2	2	6			
3	3	7			
4	1	5			
5	6	4			
6	7	1			
7	4	2			
8	5	3			
9	1	6			
10	7	4			
11	5	2			
12	6	3			
13	4	1			
14	6	7			
15	2	3			
16	4	5			
17	3	1			
18	2	7			
19	5	6			
20	3	4			
21	1	2			

From *Organizing Successful Tournaments* (3e) by John Byl, 2006, Champaign, IL: Human Kinetics.

Eight Entries at One Location

Tournament name _____

Tournament date _____

Tournament location _____

Seed 1	
Seed 2	
Seed 3	
Seed 4	
Seed 5	
Seed 6	
Seed 7	
Seed 8	

Game	Home	Away	Date	Time	Results
1	4	7			
2	1	6			
3	2	5			
4	3	8			
5	7	1			
6	6	4			
7	8	5			
8	2	7			
9	3	6			
10	4	1			
11	8	2			
12	5	7			
13	1	3			
14	4	8			
15	6	2			
16	7	3			
17	5	1			
18	8	6			
19	2	4			
20	3	5			
21	6	7			
22	1	8			
23	4	5			
24	2	3			
25	7	8			
26	5	6			
27	3	4			
28	1	2			

From *Organizing Successful Tournaments* (3e) by John Byl, 2006, Champaign, IL: Human Kinetics.

Six Entries in Two Divisions at Two Locations Shared

Tournament name _____

Tournament date _____

Tournament location 1 _____

Tournament location 2 _____

Seed	Division	Name
1	1	_____
2	2	_____
3	1	_____
4	2	_____
5	1	_____
6	2	_____

Division 1

Game	Home	Away	Location	Date	Time	Results
1	5	1	2		1	
3	3	5	2		2	
6	1	3	1		3	

Division 2

Game	Home	Away	Location	Date	Time	Results
2	6	2	1		1	
4	4	6	1		2	
5	2	4	2		3	

From *Organizing Successful Tournaments* (3e) by John Byl, 2006, Champaign, IL: Human Kinetics.

Seven Entries in Two Divisions at Two Locations Shared

Tournament name _____

Tournament date _____

Tournament location 1 _____

Tournament location 2 _____

Seed	Division	Name
1	1	_____
2	2	_____
3	1	_____
4	2	_____
5	1	_____
6	2	_____

Division 1

Game	Home	Away	Location	Date	Time	Results
1	5	1	1		1	
4	3	5	2		3	
9	1	3	1		5	

Division 2

Game	Home	Away	Location	Date	Time	Results
2	4	7	1		2	
3	2	6	1		2	
5	6	7	1		3	
6	4	6	2		4	
7	7	2	1		4	
8	2	4	2		5	

From *Organizing Successful Tournaments* (3e) by John Byl, 2006, Champaign, IL: Human Kinetics.

Eight Entries in Two Divisions at Two Locations Shared

Tournament name _____

Tournament date _____

Tournament location 1 _____

Tournament location 2 _____

Seed	Division	Name
1	1	_____
2	2	_____
3	1	_____
4	2	_____
5	1	_____
6	2	_____
7	1	_____
8	2	_____

Division 1

Game	Home	Away	Location	Date	Time	Results
1	1	5	2		1	
3	3	7	2		2	
6	7	1	1		3	
8	3	5	1		4	
10	5	7	1		5	
12	1	3	1		6	

Division 2

Game	Home	Away	Location	Date	Time	Results
2	2	6	1		1	
4	4	8	1		2	
5	8	2	2		3	
7	4	6	2		4	
9	6	8	2		5	
11	2	4	2		6	

From *Organizing Successful Tournaments* (3e) by John Byl, 2006, Champaign, IL: Human Kinetics.

Nine Entries in Two Divisions at Two Locations Shared

Tournament name _____

Tournament date _____

Tournament location 1 _____

Tournament location 2 _____

Seed	Division	Name
1	1	_____
2	2	_____
3	1	_____
4	2	_____
5	1	_____
6	2	_____
7	1	_____
8	2	_____
9	2	_____

Division 1

Game	Home	Away	Location	Date	Time	Results
3	1	5	2		2	
5	3	7	2		3	
10	7	1	1		5	
12	3	5	1		6	
14	5	7	1		7	
16	1	3	1		8	

Division 2

Game	Home	Away	Location	Date	Time	Results
1	8	9	2		1	
2	6	2	1		1	
4	9	4	1		2	
6	8	2	1		3	
7	2	9	2		4	
8	4	6	1		4	
9	6	8	2		5	
11	4	8	2		6	
13	9	6	2		7	
15	2	4	2		8	

From *Organizing Successful Tournaments* (3e) by John Byl, 2006, Champaign, IL: Human Kinetics.

Ten Entries in Two Divisions at Two Locations Shared

Tournament name _____

Tournament date _____

Tournament location 1 _____

Tournament location 2 _____

Seed	Division	Name
1	1	_____
2	2	_____
3	1	_____
4	2	_____
5	1	_____
6	2	_____
7	1	_____
8	2	_____
9	1	_____
10	2	_____

Division 1

Game	Home	Away	Location	Date	Time	Results
2	7	1	1		1	
4	9	5	1		2	
5	3	7	2		3	
7	5	1	2		4	
9	9	3	2		5	
11	5	7	2		6	
13	1	9	2		7	
16	3	5	1		8	
18	7	9	1		9	
20	1	3	1		10	

Division 2

Game	Home	Away	Location	Date	Time	Results
1	8	2	2		1	
3	10	6	2		2	
6	4	8	1		3	
10	6	2	1		4	
10	10	4	1		5	
12	6	8	1		6	
14	2	10	1		7	
15	4	6	2		8	
17	8	10	2		9	
19	2	4	2		10	

From *Organizing Successful Tournaments* (3e) by John Byl, 2006, Champaign, IL: Human Kinetics.

CHAPTER 6

Extended Tournaments

An extended tournament, as the name implies, can go on indefinitely. This type of tournament is often used for dual activities, particularly racket sports. As an ongoing tournament in intramurals or even in a physical education class, this type of tournament can be effective. Entries challenge players above them, so the schedule of games is up to the players themselves.

Though you can hold large extended tournaments, it is usually more effective to limit the size, perhaps to 15. If you have more than 15 entries, you might wish to create two or three extended tournaments, each reflecting a different level of play—perhaps with the categories of novice, intermediate, and advanced.

It is possible for this type of tournament to go on forever, but that is usually not desirable. You may want to set a time limit on the tournament or to announce at fixed times who is leading. The most popular versions of this type of tournament are the ladder and the pyramid. There are also other types that work effectively. Because these tournaments are ongoing, the participants often change their positions on the tournament board by themselves. If the extended tournament is being held in a YMCA or racket club, it might be helpful to include a phone number for each entry so players can arrange their contests.

In the case of racket clubs or intramurals, you may find that not all entries are participating, even though they signed up for the tournament. To ensure that all participants are active, you might ask players to write the date of their last game on the back of their identifying marker; you can then remove entries who have not played for a specified time (one week is usually sufficient). In a physical education class or other setting in which you want all entries to be participating, you might create rules to ensure this happens. For example, suppose two entries continually challenge each other and play no one else; a rule stating that an entry cannot play the same opponent twice in a row would solve this problem.

To ensure evenly matched games and a tournament that reflects the different calibers of play, players should play only those one or two levels removed from their level. The most common rule is that a player can play someone at a lower level only when he or she is challenged by such an entry. A second common rule is that you can challenge someone one or two levels up from yourself, but no further. If the challenger wins, he or she exchanges places with the entry they have defeated.

There are several common ways to assign initial positions to entries at the start of an extended tournament. The easiest is to assign them randomly. This encourages players to challenge each other as they rise and fall to their levels of play. Another way is to seed the entries and place them in reverse order onto the tournament sheet. With the weakest players on the top and the strongest on the bottom, the strongest are encouraged to challenge the other entries in order to move up. A third approach is to seed and place entries where you feel they should be. This decreases the number of lopsided games but provides less incentive for players to challenge each other.

Ladder Tournament

The most common extended tournament is probably the ladder. As the name implies, this tournament format looks like a ladder, with an entry on each rung. The objective is to work your way up the ladder by winning games against those higher than you.

There are many ways to construct a layout for this tournament; we list some at the end of this chapter. One suggestion is to use Popsicle sticks or tongue depressors as rungs on which you print names, as shown in figure 6.1. Make a hole in each end of each rung to place onto the hooks fastened to the uprights. Print a contestant's name and starting position on each stick to show advancement.

Figure 6.1   Ladder tournament.

Pyramid Tournament

This type of tournament is similar to the ladder tournament except that many participants may be on the same level. As in the ladder tournament, entries may only challenge one or two levels up from their positions. The advantage is that instead of a single player at the bottom, as in the ladder tournament, several players share that position. Figure 6.2 illustrates what such a tournament "bracket" would look like. A useful variation on the pyramid tournament is the crown tournament, sometimes referred to as the king tournament (figure 6.3). A crown tournament is made up of several pyramids, each with 10 spaces, at different levels. Challenging is vertical within each pyramid and horizontal among pyramids. The object is to advance as high up the pyramids as possible. You may add more pyramids to the pattern if there are enough participants.

Another variation on the pyramid tournament is a spiderweb tournament, shown in figure 6.4. The object of this tournament is to work your way as close to the center as possible. The advantage of the spiderweb is that it can accommodate more contestants in its diagram. The disadvantage is that as the center or winner's position is approached, the number of contestants remains the same as in the outer ring. In figure 6.4, eight contestants are vying for the center position and is referred to as a spiderweb tournament. This tournament forces the player in the center to play numerous matches.

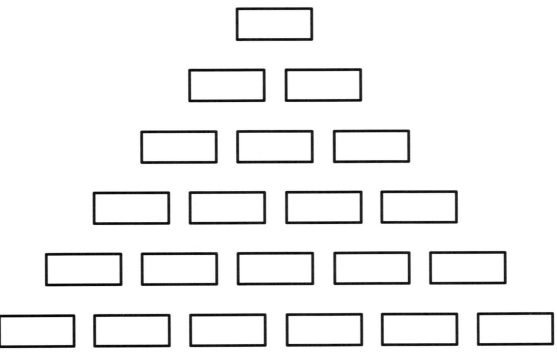

Figure 6.2   Pyramid tournament.

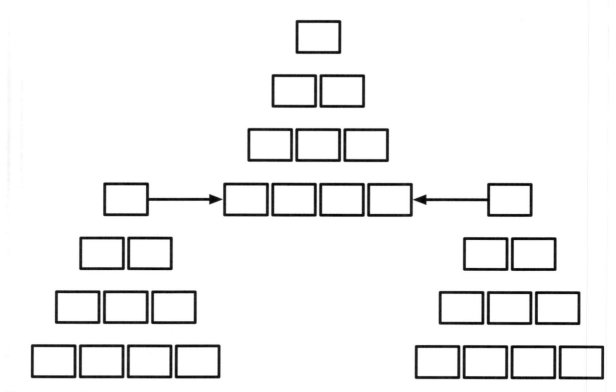

Figure 6.3 Crown tournament.

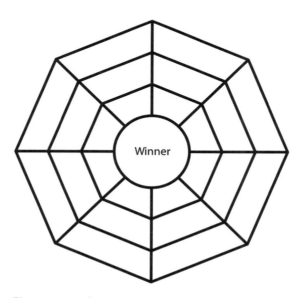

Figure 6.4 Spiderweb tournament.

Level Rotation Tournament

This type of tournament is much like the ladder except that the challenges are built in and you need keep no record of who is playing whom. This ensures that all participants play and no one is left out. This tournament type is especially helpful if the activity requires changing positions many times, as in a series of combatives or short badminton games. For example, you might wish to have students play a series of five-minute badminton games, rotating after each. In this case, a level rotation tournament structure would prove effective and easy to use, especially because you write nothing down.

The procedure is simple. When the activity is completed, the winners move one playing area over in one direction, and the losers move one playing area over in the other direction (figure 6.5). The result is that participants of similar ability play each other. In figure 6.5, the numbers refer to the players' level. The figure shows players assigned randomly in the first game. After the first game, seed number 10 has lost and thus moves to the right, as do seeds 7, 8, and 9. Players who have won—4, 3, and 2—move to the left. In the second round, the same process occurs again. After several rounds, players are playing those of like ability. There is no ultimate winner or loser, though players obviously try to move as far to the winners' side as they can.

If there is an insufficient number of playing spots, you could insert a rest spot between two playing spots.

		◄ Winners		
1	4	3	9	5
10	7	8	2	6
		Losers ►		
4	3	2	5	6
1	10	7	8	9
3	2	5	6	9
1	4	10	7	8
2	5	6	8	9
1	3	4	10	7
3	4	8	7	9
1	2	5	6	10
2	5	6	9	10
1	3	4	8	7

Figure 6.5 Level rotation tournament.

Tournament Construction

Whatever means you choose to construct these tournaments, make sure space is sufficient to accommodate all participants. You can construct the layouts for these tournaments in a way that makes them reusable, so it is usually best to build them for a large number of participants. Here are four ways of constructing layouts for extended tournaments.

- **Bulletin board.** Place the tournament format on a bulletin board, using cardboard, felt, or other materials to outline the tournament. Create little cardboard markers identifying the participants and place them on the board with pins (because of the amount of player movement that typically occurs during a tournament, use pins that you can easily insert and remove). The disadvantage is that the bulletin board is usually permanently attached to a wall, and its location might not be advantageous in relation to tournament playing areas, or it might be unprotected when not in use, which might result in accidental or intentional alteration.

- **Portable board**. This board should be large enough to accommodate the number of participants. Usually, hooks are placed on the board. Small disks identifying participants have holes punched into them so you can place the disks on the hooks. Another way to make participant identifiers is to use strips of cardboard, Popsicle sticks, or tongue depressors. This method of construction is much the same as for the bulletin board, but it has the advantage of portability.

- **Plastic or laminated surface.** Draw the tournament format with permanent markers on a sheet of paper, laminate the paper, then affix it to a firm material, such as wood or cardboard. Write participants' names using water-soluble markers. This is probably the most flexible method, though it can be messy. A less messy, but more expensive, system is to use erasable marker boards.

- **Blackboard.** Use blackboards to draw tournaments of short duration. You can make up tournaments quickly and change them as necessary. However, blackboards also are not protected when not in use, which may result in accidental or intentional alteration.

Advantages of an Extended Tournament

- You can conduct them over any length of time.
- The number of games per entry can be unlimited.
- Little supervision is required.
- No one is eliminated.

Disadvantages of an Extended Tournament

- The number of games depends on the entrants' initiative is challenging.

The best use for an extended tournament is in individual sports in recreational settings.

CHAPTER 7

Creative Tournament Solutions

In most cases the traditional formats described in this book will work well in developing the schedules you require for your tournaments and leagues. However, every once in a while circumstances challenge us to come up with variations of these schedules to create the best competitive experience for participants. In this chapter we present three of these innovative solutions, including a semi–round robin tournament, a round robin ladder tournament, and a method for dealing with very large tournaments.

Semi–Round Robin Tournaments

In a round robin tournament with seven entries, dividing the teams into two uneven divisions is a common procedure but is sometimes problematic because one division contains three entries and the other contains four. Let's first explain the normal procedure before discussing its problem and the solution provided by the semi–round robin (SRR).

In the normal procedure, the top two teams from each division play a crossover game (or match) in the semifinals, with the winners going to the championship. The division with three entries requires three games. The division with four entries requires six games. The entries in the division with three teams each play two games, whereas the division with four teams each play three games. Two problems can arise with this procedure. From a time perspective, having a division with four entries is sometimes undesirable. In competitions such as ice hockey tournaments, having one division play extra games means more ice time, which is often expensive. From a fatigue perspective, particularly for pitching rotations in baseball, this is undesirable—the finalist in the division with three entries enters the semifinals with their third pitcher and enters the finals with their fourth pitcher, whereas the finalist in the division with four entries enters the semifinals with their fourth pitcher and enters the finals with their fifth pitcher.

The number of games needs to be reduced in the larger division. One way to solve this problem is to use the SRR for the division with four entries. In division play with three entries, each entry competes twice; the same is true in the SRR format for four entries.

A SRR runs as follows:

Match 1	Entry A	Match 3	Winner of match 1
	Entry B		Winner of match 2
Match 2	Entry C	Match 4	Loser of match 1
	Entry D		Loser of match 2

There are three possible ways to match the entries in this type of tournament; the results for each type are shown in tables 7.1 to 7.3 (entries are listed by final outcome).

Table 7.1 Seeding 1–2, 3–4

Entry	Win	Lose	Entry	Win	Lose	Seed	Wins	Losses	Rank
1	X		1	X		1	2	0	1
2		X	3		X	2	1	1	2
3	X		2	X		3	1	1	3
4		X	4		X	4	0	2	4

Table 7.2 Seeding 1–3, 2–4

Entry	Win	Lose	Entry	Win	Lose	Seed	Wins	Losses	Rank
1	X		1	X		1	2	0	1
3		X	2		X	2	1	1	2
2	X		3	X		3	1	1	3
4		X	4		X	4	0	2	4

Table 7.3   Seeding 1–4, 2–3

Entry	Win	Lose	Entry	Win	Lose	Seed	Wins	Losses	Rank
1	X		1	X		1	2	0	1
4		X	2		X	2	1	1	2
2	X		3	X		3	1	1	3
3		X	4		X	4	0	2	4

No matter how the teams are seeded, the outcome of wins and losses is the same—the top entry will win both games, the second and third entries will split, and the fourth-place team will lose both games. In a SRR, the second- and third-place teams will always tie; thus, a tiebreaking procedure needs to be in place before a tournament begins. We recommend applying the following tiebreaker:

To break a tie . . .

1. Look at tied entries—who won the game between them?
2. Look at the team below the tied entries:
   a. Who has the best win–loss game ratio? (ie. In tennis, badminton...)?
   b. Who has the best plus–minus points (goals) ratio?
3. Look at the team above the tied entries:
   a. Who has the best win–loss game ratio?
   b. Who has the best plus–minus points (goals) ratio?
4. Who scored the earliest goal (point) in the game . . .
   a. Between the tied entries?
   b. In the game with the team below?
   c. In the game with the team above?

It is most satisfactory if the two teams can break a tie by playing each other. Thus, if possible, have the second and third seeds play each other in the first match (table 7.3). If seeding is not possible, that is not a problem, except that the tie between second and third might need to be broken by how well those teams did against the other two teams and not against each other. The recording sheets included on the CD seed as suggested.

A weakness of this SRR is that each game and point matters more when the second and third seeds do not play each other in the first round. This situation might cause the second- and third-place teams to beat the fourth-place team quickly and run up the score on the fourth-place team. We can eliminate this problem if we schedule the second- and third-place teams to play each other in the first round.

Table 7.4 shows when the SRR can be used. For example, with seven entries there is one division of three entries in a round robin and one division of four in a SRR. Figure 7.1 (page 123) provides a planning sheet for a semi–round robin tournament.

Table 7.4 Using the Semi–Round Robin

Number of entries	Divisions of 3 entries Round Robin	Divisions of Semi–Round Robin
7	1	1
8		2
9	3	
10	2	1
11	1	2
12	4	
13	3	1
14	2	2
15	1	3
16		4

From *Organizing Successful Tournaments* (3e) by John Byl, 2006, Champaign, IL: Human Kinetics.

In comparison to a regular round robin, the SRR offers two advantages. The first is that a SRR reduces the number of games from six to four for the division of four, which saves time and, likely, money. The second is that even when divisions are of unequal sizes (three and four), all entries still play the same number of matches before going into the playoffs. This reduction in games for one division is helpful in many sports and is critically important in baseball.

Tournament name _____

Tournament date _____

Tournament location 1 _____

Tournament location 2 _____

Seed 1	
Seed 2	
Seed 3	
Seed 4	

Game	Home	Away	Date	Time	Results
1	1	4			
2	2	3			
3	Win 1	Win 2			
4	Lose 2	Lose 1			

Entry	Win	Lose	Rank
1			
2			
3			
4			

Figure 7.1 Semi–round robin planner.

Using the Software

1. Open the Semi–Round Robin folder.
2. Open the file by the number of entries and locations. For example, SRR 8E, 2D, 1L, 1R is semi–round-robin, eight entries, two divisions, one location, competed one time through the schedule (see figures 7.2 and 7.3).
3. Fill in the competition name, competition date, seeds, locations, dates, and times, using the "tab" button to move from field to field. *Note:* If you fail to use the tab button, the field will not be entered.
4. Save the file to your hard drive.
5. Print a copy.

Game	Home	Away	Location	Date	Time	Record
2						
4						
6	Lose 2	Lose 4				
8	Win 4	Win 2				

Figure 7.2   Sample cd file—SRR, 8E, 2D, 1L, 1R, page 1.

RESULTS

Entry Name	1	2	3	4	W	T	L	Df	Ns	Pts	Rk
1		-	-	-							
2	-		-	-							
3	-	-		-							
4	-	-	-								

W=Win, T=Tie, L=Loss, Df=Default
Ns=No-show, Pts=Points, Rk=Rank

Figure 7.3   Sample cd file—SRR, 8E, 2D, 1L, 1R, page 2.

Round Robin Ladder Tournaments

After having tried various pyramid tournaments for squash at Redeemer University College, we found that not all of the 50 people who signed up were getting involved. We then set up a ladder tournament in which we indicated which entry each person should play that week. We would then move the winners up and losers down accordingly.[1] This did not work when we got to midterms and at the end of the semester when papers were due; one week was "not enough time to play" and contributed to many defaults. We wanted to give people more time to get their matches in, so we went to a series of divisions set up in a pyramid fashion. There were five people to a division, and they were to play each other once each during a four-week period. We would then move the winners to a higher division and the losers to a lower division.[2] Students and faculty being what they are, they procrastinated till the last week and then could not get all their games in; one month was "too long" and contributed to many defaults. We went to smaller divisions of three people per division, arranging one division on top of the other. This meant participants needed to get two matches in during two weeks, after which winners would move to the division above, losers would move to the division below, and those in the middle would stay put.[3] This worked for most people, the exceptions being those at the bottom of a ladder, who were looking at 50 people above them; those on the bottom began defaulting their games because there seemed little possibility of advancing far up the ladder.

We switched to a round robin–pyramid tournament, and this one seems to be working for now. We place participants in divisions of three or four people and expect them to get their games within two weeks. We place these divisions in a group of pyramids, with the top division being identified as AAAA, the next group of pyramids as AAA, then AA, and finally A. Rather than placing these groups under each other, we place them slightly below and to the right of the stronger group. Players at the different levels compete to move up in their respective pyramid, then on to the next one. This approach appears to provide the right incentives for people at all levels to stay involved. We post a sign-up sheet (see figure 7.4) beside the tournament draw so new people can sign up (they are placed at the bottom of the pyramid), and those involved can indicate if they wish to withdraw after the current round of play. If someone does not participate for two full rounds of play, we usually withdraw their name from the pyramid. If we remove someone from the pyramid, entries below the withdrawn entry move up one rung. The division sheets are included in figure 7.5 on pages 127-129. They are all set up for the AA group; to produce sheets for the other groups, simply photocopy the master and white out one of the letters. If you have more than 32 participants, form two or more major divisions to encourage those of similar ability to compete with each other. You might find this round robin–pyramid tournament will work for you. If it does not work, keep experimenting till you find a format that best suits your participants.

[1] John Byl, "Formalizing a Ladder Tournament," *NIRSA Journal* 15, no. 1 (fall 1990): 41-43.
[2] John Byl, "A Round Robin Pyramid," *NIRSA Journal* 26, no. 2 (winter 1992): 41-42.
[3] John Byl, "A Round Robin Ladder Tournament," *CAHPER Journal* 60, no. 2 (summer 1994): 25-27.

Sign-Up (and Off) List

Add my name	Delete my name	Home phone#	Work phone#	E-mail address

Figure 7.4

From *Organizing Successful Tournaments* (3e) by John Byl, 2006, Champaign, IL: Human Kinetics.

<-- 1st to CCCCC1c
<-- 2nd to CCCCC2c

Names	A	B	C	D	Wins	Place
A _____ _____		a - b a - b a - b a - b a - b	a - c a - c a - c a - c a - c	a - d a - d a - d a - d a - d		
B _____ _____	b - a b - a b - a b - a b - a		b - c b - c b - c b - c b - c	b - d b - d b - d b - d b - d		
C _____ _____	c - a c - a c - a c - a c - a	c - b c - b c - b c - b c - b		c - d c - d c - d c - d c - d		
D _____ _____	d - a d - a d - a d - a d - a	d - b d - b d - b d - b d - b	d - c d - c d - c d - c d - c			

3rd to BBBB2a-->
<-- 4th to BBBB1a

Figure 7.5

(continued)

BBBB 1

1ˢᵗ to AAAc ↑

Names	A	B	C	Wins	Place
A _____ _____		a - b a - b a - b a - b a - b	a - c a - c a - c a - c a - c		
B _____ _____	b - a b - a b - a b - a b - a		b - c b - c b - c b - c b - c		
C _____ _____	c - a c - a c - a c - a c - a	c - b c - b c - b c - b c - b			

3ʳᵈ to CCCC2a-->

CCCC 1

1ˢᵗ to BBBB1c ↑

Names	A	B	C	Wins	Place
A _____ _____		a - b a - b a - b a - b a - b	a - c a - c a - c a - c a - c		
B _____ _____	b - a b - a b - a b - a b - a		b - c b - c b - c b - c b - c		
C _____ _____	c - a c - a c - a c - a c - a	c - b c - b c - b c - b c - b			

3ʳᵈ to AAAa-->

↑
1st to AAAAd

Names	A	B	C	Wins	Place
A _____ _____		a - b a - b a - b a - b a - b	a - c a - c a - c a - c a - c		
B _____ _____	b - a b - a b - a b - a b - a		b - c b - c b - c b - c b - c		
C _____ _____	c - a c - a c - a c - a c - a	c - b c - b c - b c - b c - b			

<-- 3rd to CCCC1a

↑
1st to BBBB2c

Names	A	B	C	Wins	Place
A _____ _____		a - b a - b a - b a - b a - b	a - c a - c a - c a - c a - c		
B _____ _____	b - a b - a b - a b - a b - a		b - c b - c b - c b - c b - c		
C _____ _____	c - a c - a c - a c - a c - a	c - b c - b c - b c - b c - b			

3rd to AAAb-->

Figure 7.5

Using the Software

1. Open the Round Robin Ladder folder.
2. Open the file by the number of entries and locations (either 4–16 entries or 17–32 entries).
3. Fill in the entries' names in the appropriate spots on the schedule.
4. Save the file to your hard drive.
5. Print a copy.
6. Open the file Competitors' List.
7. Write all the names of the entries, sort the list alphabetically with Word (click the Table tab and scroll down to Sort).
8. Save the file to your hard drive.
9. Print a hard copy.
10. Open the file Sign-Up (and Off) List.
11. Type in the date of the start of the next tournament.
12. Save the file to your hard drive.
13. Print a hard copy.

Very Large Tournaments

It is best to think of a large tournament as a series of smaller divisions. Some divisions will occur naturally. For example, you might receive 100 entries for a high school badminton tournament, but they are divided into five categories: men's singles and doubles, women's singles and doubles, and mixed doubles. There may also be a junior and senior division, making 10 different tournaments with an average of 10 entries per category. You would then prepare an appropriate format for each category.

However, you might at times encounter a situation in which you have many teams in a single category. A large two-on-two basketball tournament might have 100 entries. One solution would be to divide these 100 entries into 16 divisions, resulting in 12 divisions of six teams and 4 divisions of seven teams. Each entry would play the other entries in their division. You would place the top two finishers from each division (a total of 32) on a different single-elimination playoff draw, so these two entries would not meet again unless they made it to the championships. Seed entries so each number-one finisher plays a second-place finisher from division play. Each single-elimination draw would end up with a winner and a second-place finisher. The second-place finishers from the two draws would play for third and fourth overall. The two first-place finishers from the two draws would play in the championship match for first and second overall. Calculations to figure the total number of games to complete this whole tournament go like this:

Division Play

12 divisions of 6

$$12 \times (6 \times [6 - 1] / 2) = 180 \text{ games}$$

4 divisions of 7

$$4 \times (7 \times [7 - 1] / 2) = 84 \text{ games}$$

Single-elimination playoffs

$$2 \times (16 - 1) = 30$$

Consolation and championships = 2 games

Total = 296 games

If you had 24 courts, it would take . . .

17 rounds to complete division play,

4 rounds to complete the playoffs,

1 round to complete the consolation and championship game, and

22 rounds to complete the tournament.

If each game (or match) lasted 30 minutes, the tournament would last 11 hours, and the fewest games anyone would play would be five. See figure 7.6.

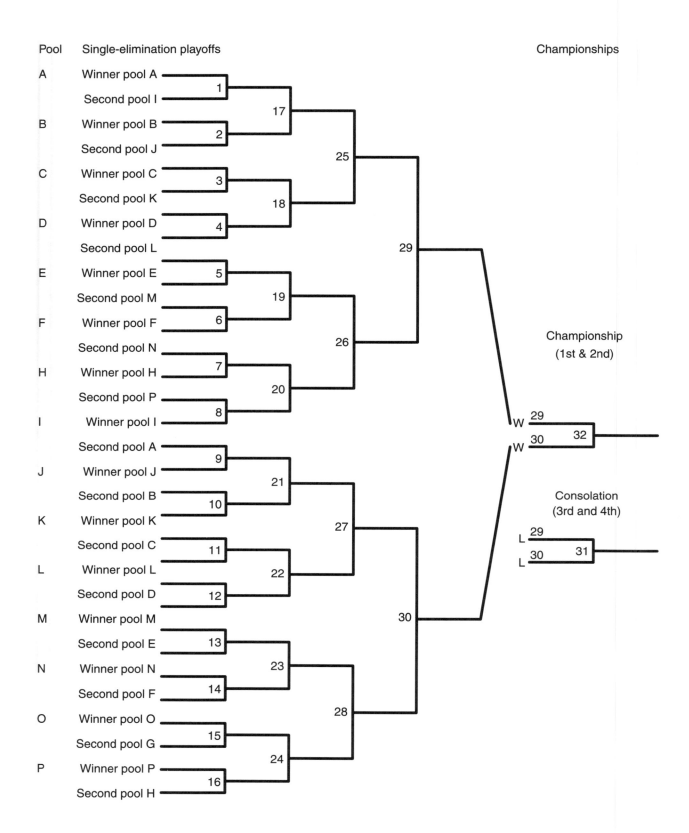

Figure 7.6 Single-elimination schematic.

CHAPTER 8

Seeding and Byes

The concepts of seeding and byes are important to understand in preparing a successful tournament. For this manual we have prepared seeding charts, which include byes, for each type of tournament, adding ease and accuracy to the tournament director's job. However, if you want to understand how to do seeding, this chapter will interest you. Also, for situations in which it is helpful to seed but the entries have not played each other, this chapter concludes with suggestions for dealing with that.

Understanding Byes

The first round of a single-elimination, double-elimination, or multilevel tournament is always calculated to the next-higher perfect power of two. In other words, the initial round allows for up to 2, 4, 6, 16, 32, or 64 entries. You might ask, what happens if I have less than that? What happens if I have seven entries? Obviously, the format permitting only four entries would be too small for seven, so a format using eight entries would be necessary. This means that one entry will not have anyone to play in the first round; in such a case, that entry receives what is called a bye.

Two principles are usually applied in awarding a bye. First, the number-one seed or the higher seeds should be overcome by skillful play and not by the exhaustion that can come from a difficult schedule. Second, lower-caliber players benefit most from more experience and playing with those of similar ability. Thus, byes are usually awarded to the higher-ranked entries. We illustrate this in figure

8.1, using a single-elimination draw sheet for seven entries. If you are preparing a single-elimination tournament with six entries, then two entries receive byes. These should be the number-one and number-two seeds.

The process of awarding byes is slightly different in round robin play. In a regular round robin, when there is an odd number of entries, each entry has one bye built into the schedule. In the case of split round robins, if the divisions are not all the same size, entries in smaller divisions play fewer games; these are not normally referred to as byes, but byes are essentially what those entries are receiving.

Assigning Seeds

As we discussed in chapter 1, when organizing a tournament, especially an elimination tournament, two important principles should be at work in preparing the draw. The first is that the top two entries should meet in the final game; a logical extension of this is that the higher an entry is ranked, the closer it should come to the final game before being eliminated.

A second principle, which is applied differently depending on the seeding philosophy you adopt, is that it should be equally difficult for entries of similar ability to achieve similar ends. Let's illustrate this point with a tournament of 16 entries (see figures 8.1 and 8.2). Using the equitable seeding approach, the 1st seed competes with the 10th seed, and the 2nd seed competes with the 11th seed—both 9 seeds apart. Using the advantage seeding approach, the 1st seed competes with the 16th, and the 2nd seed competes with the 15th; the higher seed plays the easiest competitor, and the second seed plays the second easiest competitor. The benefits of the equitable seeding approach are as follows:

- The weaker teams should have more meaningful games (although they will likely still be eliminated in the same round that they would be eliminated in if playing in an advantage seeded tournament).
- There should be fewer and less lopsided games than in an advantage seeded tournament.

The benefit of the advantage seeding approach is as follows:

- The stronger teams have earned (usually as the result of previous league or round robin competition) an easier path to their final games, and these earnings are accommodated by this seeding approach.

The easiest way to understand seeding is to apply these two principles from the end of a tournament format to its beginning. Figure 8.3 illustrates such an application using the equitable seeding approach. Seed 1 should win this tournament and thus is placed at the end as the winner. To earn that spot, seed 1 should have played seed 2 in the final game; seed 1 and seed 2 represent the winners of the two similar brackets, so they advance to play each other. The semifinals should include four teams; remaining consistent with our first principle, this should include the top four entries. Who the first and second seeds play is decided by a third principle. If we applied the second principle (about equal difficulty in advancing) properly, then seed 1 would play seed 3, and seed 2 would play seed 4. The problem here is that the third seed is closer to seed 2 than seed 4 and

Starting position	Number of entries													
	3	4	5	6	7	8	9	10	11	12	13	14	15	16
A	1	1	1	1	1	1	1	1	1	1	1	1	1	1
B	B	4	B	B	B	8	B	B	B	B	B	B	B	16
C	3	3	5	5	5	5	9	9	9	9	9	9	9	9
D	2	2	4	4	4	4	8	8	8	8	8	8	8	8
E			3	3	3	3	5	5	5	5	5	5	5	5
F			B	6	6	6	B	B	B	12	12	12	12	12
G			B	B	7	7	B	B	B	B	13	13	13	13
H			2	2	2	2	4	4	4	4	4	4	4	4
I							3	3	3	3	3	3	3	3
J							B	B	B	B	B	14	14	14
K							B	B	11	11	11	11	11	11
L							6	6	6	6	6	6	6	6
M							7	7	7	7	7	7	7	7
N							B	10	10	10	10	10	10	10
O							B	B	B	B	B	B	15	15
P							2	2	2	2	2	2	2	2

Figure 8.1 Advantage seeding for single- and double-elimination tournaments.

Starting position	Number of entries												
	4	5	6	7	8	9	10	11	12	13	14	15	16
A	1	1	1	1	1	1	1	1	1	1	1	1	1
B	4	B	B	B	6	B	B	B	B	B	B	B	10
C	3	5	5	5	5	B	B	10	11	12	13	14	15
D	2	4	4	4	4	6	6	6	6	6	6	6	6
E		3	3	3	3	5	5	5	5	5	5	5	5
F		B	6	7	8	B	B	B	10	11	12	13	14
G		B	B	6	7	B	B	B	B	10	11	12	13
H		2	2	2	2	4	4	4	4	4	4	4	4
I						3	3	3	3	3	3	3	3
J						B	B	B	B	B	10	11	12
K						9	9	9	9	9	9	9	9
L						8	8	8	8	8	8	8	8
M						7	7	7	7	7	7	7	7
N						B	10	11	12	13	14	15	16
O						B	B	B	B	B	B	10	11
P						2	2	2	2	2	2	2	2

Figure 8.2 Equitable seeding for single-elimination and multilevel tournaments.

should have the opportunity to give seed 2 the best challenge for the championship game. Thus, seed 1 played seed 4, and seed 2 played seed 3; this seeding also gives the top seed an easier game.

Going to the first round, seed 1 is awarded a bye, and seeds 5, 6, and 7 are added to the draw sheet. If you use the principles consistently, the following would occur: Seed 3 would play seed 6, seed 4 would play seed 7, and seed 2 would play seed 5. Each entry would play someone three seeds away, but this scenario would create a considerable disadvantage for seed 5. The difference between the fourth and fifth seeds might also be minimal. However, the only way the fifth seed can break into the semifinals, if we seeded as suggested, would be by defeating an entry seeded three levels ahead. Thus, we altered the seeding for the fifth, sixth, and seventh seeds as indicated in figure 8.3.

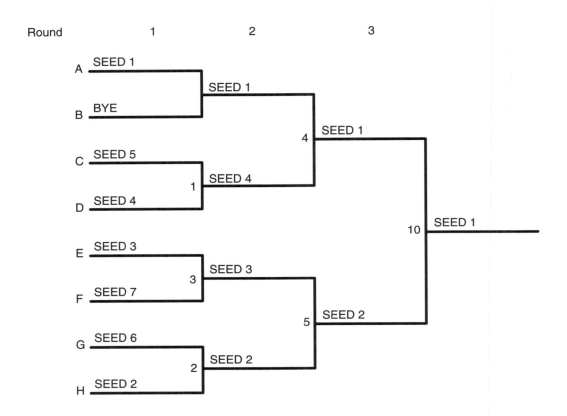

Figure 8.3 Single-elimination tournament with equitable seeding and a bye for the top-ranked entrant.

Figure 8.4 indicates how improper seeding leads to an unjust process and unjust results. With respect to the first principle, the top two seeds did make it to the finals, but in the semifinals, round 2, seed 6 made it to the semifinals but seed 3 did not; this is an undesirable result. With respect to the second principle, a quick look at the playing schedules for the top two seeds indicates a discrepancy. In the case of the second seed, a bye is awarded, a game is played with the sixth seed, then the second seed is into the finals. By contrast, the top seed played the third seed, then the fourth seed, then played the second seed in the finals. Obviously seed 1 had a much more difficult schedule than seed 2 did, and that is likely to be a disadvantage to seed 1.

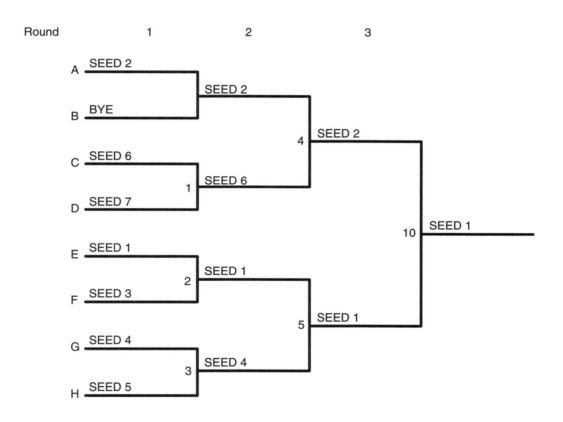

Figure 8.4   Single-elimination tournament with improper seeding.

Occasionally, you may not have the information to know the caliber of each entry, which makes specific seeding difficult. The best solution to this problem is to rank the top quarter of the entries, then divide the remaining entries in half, classifying one group as average and the other as weak. For example, suppose there are eight entries and you can clearly identify the top two, and you can divide the remaining six into two groups: three in the average group and three in the weak group. Place the three in the average group on the draw sheet where the third, fourth, and fifth seeds would be; then place the weak group on the draw sheet where the sixth, seventh, and eighth seeds would be. It is especially important to seed the top teams correctly; after doing that, seed the remaining entries as best as possible.

We must add that, in some sports and leagues, rules specify that the tournament director may seed only a certain number of entries and must simply place the remaining entries onto the draw sheet at random. For example, international badminton regulations do not permit seeding more than 2 entries when there are less than 16 players, and no more than 4 entries when the total is less than 32. Eight seeded entries are the maximum allowed.

Using the seeding tables in this manual (or tables you have developed yourself), you may have scheduled two players from the same club or city to play each other. On most occasions this is undesirable, and you might need to slightly modify the seeding order by placing these players in different brackets or divisions. When using the CD, once you type in the divisions they will automatically be listed beside the seed name. You might need to adjust some teams on the CD seeding list to avoid having two entries from a similar place being assigned to the same division.

Seeding Entries Who Have Not Played Each Other

It is always helpful to seed entries to minimize mismatches and to allow for the top four teams to meet in the semifinals and the top two teams to meet in the finals. If seeding is based on a season of play, the final league standings provide the basis of seeding. However, it commonly occurs that a tournament convener is hosting a tournament in which the entries have not played each other. If this is the case, how does one seed the entries?

The most likely place for this situation to occur is in a preseason exhibition tournament. It might also occur in a championship competition in which the entries have local competitions advancing a winner to regional or larger tournaments. Examples of the latter include high school provincial or state tournaments or Olympic competitions.

A typical safeguard in such situations is to provide a preliminary round of round robin divisional play. For example, if you have 16 entries, you might divide the entries into four divisions of four. Based on the results of divisional play, you could then seed a 16-entry single-elimination playoff.

But even if you used this safeguard, how could you ensure the best matchups even in divisional play? Basically, there are three ways to try to do this:

1. See how these teams (or players) fared in games they played against each other, if any, or against a common team in exhibition or qualifying games.
2. Evaluate historical patterns.
3. Ask experts who have seen these entries compete.

If teams (or players) have played each other before the tournament, those results can factor into the seeding. Two teams might not have played each other, but perhaps they both played another team. How the two teams did against the other team can indicate relative strength. If the Lions beat the Bears, and the Bears beat the Cougars, and the Lions and the Cougars are coming to the same tournament, the Lions would be seeded higher than the Cougars.

Historically, some teams (or players) are very good every year, and this information can be used for seeding purposes. Similarly, teams from certain locations might be traditionally strong or weak in certain sports, and this information too might be helpful during seeding. In addition, if teams in a tournament have not played in previous tournaments during the year, their rankings from the previous year might be used to help with seeding, though such information can be misleading, especially with school teams, whose caliber of play might change dramatically from year to year because of graduation.

A tournament convener should be willing to ask around to see how teams are doing. Coaches could be asked to comment on their team's relative strength from previous years. Coaches might also be able to comment on what they have heard about other teams.

Probably no one approach will solve the problem of accurate seeding for teams that have not played each other for a considerable time. However, all that is asked of tournament conveners is that they do the best they can. Providing a preliminary round of divisional play is probably the safest thing to do. In addition, a careful look at the entries' history of play will help make for a good tournament.

A tournament director seeds with the best information and intentions, but upsets do occur. This is part of the fun of a tournament. As tournament director, do not feel bad if your high seeds lose early. Rather, feel good about preparing and hosting a tournament that you have seeded as fairly as possible given the information you had.

CHAPTER 9

Tiebreaking Procedures

From time to time, a game or match needs to have a winner and cannot be left as a tie. The first part of this chapter gives examples of how that can be done. In the case of round robin tournaments or league play, it might also be necessary to break a tie for purposes of final standings. The second part of this chapter explains how that can be done.

Tiebreaking Procedures for Games

You should use tiebreaking procedures only when the outcome of a game determines which entry advances or when knowing the final standings is necessary. We have also listed alternative procedures. A common alternative that works for most sports is to advance the entry that scored the first point. Another alternative when all else fails is to resort to a coin toss.

Archery

The tie is broken for individuals or teams by determining who has the greatest number of 10s, then the greatest number of 9s.

Alternative

Use a single arrow shoot-off for the highest score to a maximum of three. If the score is still tied, the shooter of the arrow that is closest to the center wins.

Badminton

Women's singles games are played to 11; all other games are played to 15. If the score is tied just before the final point, the player who achieved the leading point first chooses whether the game is not set (the game goes on to 11 or 15) or the game is set, which would be as follows:

	Score	Set to
Women	9–9	3
	10–10	2
Men	13–13	5
	14–14	3

Baseball and Softball

Play continues until the visiting team has scored more total runs than the home team at the end of a completed inning, or the home team scores the winning run in an uncompleted inning.

Basketball

Following a one-minute intermission, an extra period is played. If the score is still tied, repeat this procedure until the tie is broken.

Alternative

Using free throw shooting, each team selects five players at the conclusion of the game and alternates shooting free throws. If before both teams have taken five free throws one team has scored more than the other, shooting shall cease. If the score is still tied after all 10 players have taken their free throws, this shooting shall continue one player at a time until (after an equal number of shots) one team has scored one more basket than the other.

Field Hockey

In field hockey you can break a tie multiple ways.

- Following a 5-minute rest, a 10-minute sudden victory (first goal wins) overtime period shall be played.
- Penalty strokes are taken.
- Each team selects five players from those who were on the field at the conclusion of the game. The teams alternate strokes.
- If before both teams have taken five strokes one team has scored more than the other could the score is still tied, teams shall send one player out at a time to take penalty strokes until one player from one team scores and the player from the other team does not score.

Football

Use a 10-minute intermission followed by a 20-minute overtime period of two 10-minute halves. If the score is still tied, use the same procedure but with a 5-minute intermission.

Alternative

Teams alternate kicking field goals beginning from the 20-yard line. Each time both teams complete their kicks, the ball is moved back an additional 10 yards. If both teams miss, another kick is taken from the same spot. If one team completes the kick and the other fails, the team whose kick was successful wins.

Golf

Play one to three extra playoff holes. If there is still a tie, continue to play until a player wins the hole and thus the tournament.

Ice Hockey

Use a 10-minute intermission followed by a 20-minute sudden-death overtime period. If the score is still tied, repeat the same procedure until one team scores a goal.

Alternative

Five players from each team alternate taking penalty shots. If both nets are used, teams can shoot at the same time. The puck is taken from center ice, and the player may stickhandle in and take one shot. If before both teams have taken five shots one team has scored more goals than the other could score even if it were to complete its five shots, shots shall cease. If the score is still tied after all 10 players have shot, shots shall continue one player at a time until (after an equal number of shots) one team has scored one more goal than the other.

Lacrosse (Box)

Use a 10-minute intermission followed by a 10-minute stop-time overtime period, or use a 10-minute intermission followed by a 20-minute sudden-death overtime period. Repeat the latter procedure until a goal is scored.

Lacrosse (Field)

Use a 5-minute intermission followed by two 4-minute periods, or use a 1-minute intermission followed by 4-minute periods of sudden-death competition.

Racquetball

Unlike other racket sports, a player does not need to win by 2 points. The first player to 15 points wins the game. The first entry to win two games is the winner of the match. If a third game is required, it is played to 11 points.

Rugby

Use a 10-minute overtime period, 5 minutes played each way. If the score is still tied, 5-minute periods each way are continued, but they are now sudden death.

Alternative

You can also use kicks at the goal, starting at the 22-meter line and moving out until (after an equal number of kicks) one team has missed one more than the other team.

Soccer

In soccer you can break a tie multiple ways.

- Penalty kicks are taken.
- Each team selects five players from those who were on the field at the conclusion of the game. Teams alternate kicks.
- If before both teams have taken five kicks one team has scored more than the other could score even if it were to complete its five kicks, kicks shall cease.

If the score is still tied after all 10 players have kicked, kicks shall continue one player at a time until (after an equal number of shots) one team has scored one more goal than the other.

Alternative

Use the same process except that a player takes the ball from quarterfield, dribbles toward the goal, and takes one shot. Or you can count the number of corner kicks taken during the game. Assume that the team with the most corner kicks had the most aggressive play at the other team's net, and you could thus declare them the winner.

Squash

If the score is tied 8 to 8, the receiver shall choose one of these two options:

1. No set—game played to 9 points
2. Set—game played to 10 points

United States rules have games going to 15 with setting done as in badminton.

Table Tennis

A game shall be won by the player or team first scoring 11 points unless both players or teams score 10 points, when the game shall be won by the first player or team leading by 2 points.

Tennis

A game must be won by a margin of two points. A set must be won by a margin of two games.

Alternative

A player who first wins seven points shall win the game and the set, provided he or she leads by at least two points. The player whose turn it is to serve shall serve first. The opponent shall serve the second and third serve; then players alternate every two serves. Players should change ends following every six points. In doubles play, the player whose turn it is to serve shall take the first serve. Thereafter, each player shall serve two serves, rotating as in regular games.

Volleyball

A game must be won by 2 points until one team scores 25. Matches are best two out of three or best three out of five.

Wrestling

In wrestling you can break a tie multiple ways.

- Greatest number of technical points wins;
- most 5-point moves wins,
- most 3-point moves wins,
- most 2-point moves wins, or least number of cautions wins.

Tiebreaking Procedures for Tournaments

Follow these steps in the order presented until a tie is broken. We have provided figure 9.1 (page 146) for ease of record keeping and table 9.1 for ease of ratio calculations. To use table 9.1 (page 147), enter from the left the number of games played and from the top the number of games won. The correct percentage is given at the point where the appropriate row and column intersect. You could also use this figure to calculate other percentages in which the basic numbers do not exceed 30.

If two or more entries are tied in points at the end of a league schedule or tournament, use the following to break a tie:

- Considering only the record of tied entries, rank the entry highest that has achieved one of the following:

  1. Has defeated the other(s)
  2. Has the best win–loss ratio of matches
  3. Has the best win–loss ratio of games (in games such as badminton or volleyball)
  4. Has the best goals (points) for–against ratio

- If a tie still exists, then consider only the record of tied entries with the entries below or above, give the highest rank to the entry that has achieved one of the following:

  1. Defeated the entry below or above if the other(s) did not
  2. Has the best win–loss ratio of games against the entry below or

above

3. Has the best goals (points) for–against ratio with the entry below or above compared to the other tied entries

Note: The sequence of tiebreaking a three-way tie is illustrated here:

Tied position	Sequence of entries to consider
1st	4, 5, 6, 7, 8
2nd	5, 1, 6, 7, 8
3rd	6, 2, 7, 1, 8
4th	7, 3, 8, 2, 1
5th	8, 4, 3, 2, 1
6th	5, 4, 3, 2, 1

- If a tie still exists, the tournament director shall determine the method of breaking it.

Note: If three or more teams or competitors are tied for an event place, determine the highest position by the previous procedures. Break the tie for the next

Entry Name	Matches for	Matches against	Matches total	Games for	Games against	Games total	Points	Final place
A								
B								
C								
D								
E								
F								
G								
H								
I								
J								
K								
L								
M								
N								
O								
P								

Figure 9.1 Tourney summary recording sheet.

From *Organizing Successful Tournaments* (3e) by John Byl, 2006, Champaign, IL: Human Kinetics.

Table 9.1 Determining Percent of Games Won

Games played	\ Games won → 1	2	3	4	5	6	7	8	9	10	11	12	13	14	15
30	3.33	6.67	10.00	13.33	16.67	20.00	23.33	26.67	30.00	33.33	36.67	40.00	43.33	46.67	50.00
29	3.45	6.90	10.34	13.79	17.24	20.69	24.14	27.59	31.03	34.48	37.93	41.38	44.83	48.28	51.72
28	3.57	7.14	10.71	14.29	17.86	21.43	25.00	28.57	32.14	35.71	39.29	42.86	46.43	50.00	53.57
27	3.70	7.41	11.11	14.81	18.52	22.22	25.93	29.63	33.33	37.04	40.74	44.44	48.15	51.85	55.56
26	3.85	7.69	11.54	15.38	19.23	23.08	26.92	30.77	34.62	38.46	42.31	46.15	50.00	53.85	57.69
25	4.00	8.00	12.00	16.00	20.00	24.00	28.00	32.00	36.00	40.00	44.00	48.00	52.00	56.00	60.00
24	4.17	8.33	12.50	16.67	20.83	25.00	29.17	33.33	37.50	41.67	45.83	50.00	54.17	58.33	62.50
23	4.35	8.70	13.04	17.39	21.74	26.09	30.43	34.78	39.13	43.48	47.83	52.17	56.52	60.87	65.22
22	4.55	9.09	13.64	18.18	22.73	27.27	31.82	36.36	40.91	45.45	50.00	54.55	59.09	63.64	68.18
21	4.76	9.52	14.29	19.05	23.81	28.57	33.33	38.10	42.86	47.62	52.38	57.14	61.90	66.67	71.43
20	5.00	10.00	15.00	20.00	25.00	30.00	35.00	40.00	45.00	50.00	55.00	60.00	65.00	70.00	75.00
19	5.26	10.53	15.79	21.05	26.32	31.58	36.84	42.11	47.37	52.63	57.89	63.16	68.42	73.68	78.95
18	5.56	11.11	16.67	22.22	27.78	33.33	38.89	44.44	50.00	55.56	61.11	66.67	72.22	77.78	83.33
17	5.88	11.76	17.65	23.53	29.41	35.29	41.18	47.06	52.94	58.82	64.71	70.59	76.47	82.35	88.24
16	6.25	12.50	18.75	25.00	31.25	37.50	43.75	50.00	56.25	62.50	68.75	75.00	81.25	87.50	93.75
15	6.67	13.33	20.00	26.67	33.33	40.00	46.67	53.33	60.00	66.67	73.33	80.00	86.67	93.33	100.00
14	7.14	14.29	21.43	28.57	35.71	42.86	50.00	57.14	64.29	71.43	78.57	85.71	92.86	100.00	
13	7.69	15.38	23.08	30.77	38.46	46.15	53.85	61.54	69.23	76.92	84.62	92.31	100.00		
12	8.33	16.67	25.00	33.33	41.67	50.00	58.33	66.67	75.00	83.33	91.67	100.00			
11	9.09	18.18	27.27	36.36	45.45	54.55	63.64	72.73	81.82	90.91	100.00				
10	10.00	20.00	30.00	40.00	50.00	60.00	70.00	80.00	90.00	100.00					
9	11.11	22.22	33.33	44.44	55.56	66.67	77.78	88.89	100.00						
8	12.50	25.00	37.50	50.00	62.50	75.00	87.50	100.00							
7	14.29	28.57	42.86	57.14	71.43	85.71	100.00								
6	16.67	33.33	50.00	66.67	83.33	100.00									
5	20.00	40.00	60.00	80.00	100.00										
4	25.00	50.00	75.00	100.00											
3	33.33	66.67	100.00												
2	50.00	100.00													
1	100.00														

Games played	\ Games won → 16	17	18	19	20	21	22	23	24	25	26	27	28	29	30
30	53.33	56.67	60.00	63.33	66.67	70.00	73.33	76.67	80.00	83.33	86.67	90.00	93.33	96.67	100.00
29	55.17	58.62	62.07	65.52	68.97	72.41	75.86	79.31	82.76	86.21	89.66	93.10	96.55	100.00	
28	57.14	60.71	64.29	67.86	71.43	75.00	78.57	82.14	85.71	89.29	92.86	96.43	100.00		
27	59.26	62.96	66.67	70.37	74.07	77.78	81.48	85.19	88.89	92.59	96.30	100.00			
26	61.54	65.38	69.23	73.08	76.92	80.77	84.62	88.46	92.31	96.15	100.00				
25	64.00	68.00	72.00	76.00	80.00	84.00	88.00	92.00	96.00	100.00					
24	66.67	70.83	75.00	79.17	83.33	87.50	91.67	95.83	100.00						
23	69.57	73.91	78.26	82.61	86.96	91.30	95.65	100.00							
22	72.73	77.27	81.82	86.36	90.91	95.45	100.00								
21	76.19	80.95	85.71	90.48	95.24	100.00									
20	80.00	85.00	90.00	95.00	100.00										
19	84.21	89.47	94.74	100.00											
18	88.89	94.44	100.00												
17	94.12	100.00													
16	100.00														

position applying the tiebreaking procedure from the beginning.

Figures 9.2 and 9.3 show how the tiebreaking procedure works in the case of a round robin tournament with eight entries. Figure 9.2 shows the results of an eight-entry volleyball tournament. Figure 9.3 provides the summary for this tournament.

As you can see in the points column of figure 9.3, three teams tied for second place and three teams tied for sixth place. When possible, it is best to determine the highest entry first, so we will do that.

Step 1 asks us to consider the record of matches won and lost between the tied entries. Because C beat G, G beat H, and H beat C, the tie is still not broken. The ratio of games won and lost also does not help in this case because all three entries won two games and lost two games in play between them. The third step has us look at the ratio of games won and lost considering all matches between the tied entries. Once again, each of the three entries under consideration has the same record: two matches for and two matches against. The points for and against ratio is also the same. The tie cannot be broken by looking only at the tied entries.

We then go to the second level and consider how these three teams did against the entry immediately below them: fifth place B. All three entries defeated B by the same number of matches, games, and points, so this comparison does not break the tie. We then consider how these three teams did against the entry immediately above them. In this case, all three entries were defeated by E in the same number of matches, games, and points, so this comparison does not break the tie. We cannot compare these three tied entries with the team two places below them—we do not know who that is because there is a three-way tie for that position. We will need to break that tie first.

In this case, A beat D, D beat F, and F beat A; this does not break the tie. The tie is also not broken when comparing total number of matches, games, or points between these three tied entries. We would then consider how they did with the team immediately below them. However, because there is no team immediately below them, we will look at how they did with the team immediately above them: entry B. Entry B defeated all three entries by the same number of matches and games. However, when comparing points for and against, A lost to B by a total of 2–30, D also lost by a total of 2–30, and F lost by a total of 3–30. Entry F's ratio is better than the other two and thus is awarded sixth place. To determine who receives seventh and eighth place, we start from the first step again. Because A beat D, A is awarded seventh place and D is awarded eighth place.

Now that we have determined the sixth place, we can return to see how the entries tied for second place did against this entry (entry F). We see that each of these entries defeated F. However, F did manage to win one game against H. The win–loss ratio for these teams is as shown in figure 9.4. Because H has the lowest ratio, H receives fourth place. Starting the tiebreaking procedure again from the beginning, we see that C beat G, so C is awarded second place and G is awarded third place.

	A	B	C	D	E	F	G	H	Total wins	Final place
A		1-15 1-15	1-15 1-15	15-1 15-1	0-15 0-15	1-15 1-15	1-15 1-15	1-15 1-15	1	7
B	15-1 15-1		1-15 1-15	15-1 15-1	0-15 0-15	15-1 15-2	1-15 1-15	1-15 1-15	3	5
C	15-1 15-1	15-1 15-1		15-1 15-1	0-15 0-15	15-1 15-1	15-1 15-1	1-15 1-15	5	2
D	1-15 1-15	1-15 1-15	1-15 1-15		0-15 0-15	15-1 15-1	1-15 1-15	1-15 1-15	1	8
E	15-0 15-0	15-0 15-0	15-0 15-0	15-0 15-0		15-0 15-0	15-0 15-0	15-0 15-0	7	1
F	15-1 15-1	1-15 2-15	1-15 1-15	1-15 1-15	0-15 0-15		1-15 1-15	15-1 1-15 1-15	1	6
G	15-1 15-1	15-1 15-1	1-15 1-15	15-1 15-1	0-15 0-15	15-1 15-1		15-1 15-1	5	3
H	15-1 15-1	15-1 15-1	15-1 15-1	15-1 15-1	0-15 0-15	1-15 15-1 15-1	1-15 1-15		5	4

Figure 9.2 Sample results of an eight-entry round robin volleyball tournament.

Entry name	Matches for	Matches against	Matches total	Games for	Games against	Games total	Points	Final place
A	1	6	7	2	12	14	1	7
B	3	4	7	6	8	14	3	5
C	5	2	7	10	4	14	5	2
D	1	6	7	2	12	14	1	8
E	7	0	7	14	0	14	7	1
F	1	6	7	3	12	15	1	6
G	5	2	7	10	4	14	5	3
H	5	2	7	10	5	15	5	4
I								
J								
K								
L								
M								
N								
O								
P								

Figure 9.3 Sample tourney record sheet.

Entry	Games won	Games lost	Games played	Ratio
C	2	0	2	100.00
G	2	0	2	100.00
H	2	1	3	66.67

Figure 9.4   Sample summary of games won and lost against F.

CHAPTER 10

Planning and Conducting Tournaments

The tournament director is responsible for ensuring that a tournament runs efficiently for all involved—players, officials, and spectators alike. Selecting the appropriate tournament type and seeding accurately will help a great deal. However, many other administrative activities can make a tournament run smoothly. Many times, an association will have specifications or requirements for some activities, such as by which date participants need to submit entry forms or when you should mail tournament schedules. These associations often also specify tiebreaking procedures and other items relevant for a smooth-running tournament. If other people have not taken care of these items, you should find the information in this chapter quite useful.

For large tournaments, it is helpful to delegate work to various committees that report back to the tournament director or tournament executive committee. For smaller tournaments, the director may be able to run the tournament with help from select people. For very small tournaments, a director may organize and administer the entire tournament. We have provided a checklist so you can check off items as they are completed. The time line is suitable for a midsize tournament, so you might need to lengthen or shorten it depending on the number of entries in your tournament.

Planning Ahead

When organizing tournaments, adequate planning and getting things done early are crucial to avoiding problems. It is helpful to know what tasks need to be done in what time frame. The 10 tips below should help you stay on time and plan properly. A few additional words of advice might further minimize potential problems. Use figure 10.1 (page 154), the tournament checklist, as a reference as you create your own tournament "to-do" list. Copy it off and post it near your desk so it's handy as you plan your tournament.

You will need to adjust the time line according to the nature of your tournament. For large tournaments, you should begin organizing much sooner; for less formal tournaments, the time constraints are not as applicable. In any large tournament for which you are using committees, you should activate the committees from the start. See the Assigning Committee Responsibilities section later in the chapter.

1. Obtain a written confirmation of facility bookings as early as possible. Without it, no scheduling can really begin, and having it in writing helps prevent misunderstandings with the facility director.

2. Select an appropriate playing schedule. Based on the number of entries and the objectives of your tournament, select a playing schedule from the previous chapters. Then you can develop an appropriate time schedule for tournament day.

3. Book all of the officials. Do this early or you risk not acquiring the quality of officials you want; worse yet, you might find none available. Schedule major officials, first-aid personnel, and any official security personnel you require.

4. Advise teams (or players) of the tournament details. Everyone appreciates knowing the logistics, such as playing schedule, tiebreaking procedures, specific equipment that is required (e.g., in badminton the type of shuttlecock to use). It is also helpful to provide maps clearly showing the locations of the playing facility, suitable accommodations, and restaurants. Two maps might be required: a large-scale map showing major routes to the playing site and a small-scale map showing the local area. Copy these to use in subsequent tournaments.

Participants also need to know what will be provided or available at the tournament, such as game or practice balls, refreshments, towels, first-aid supplies or personnel, and snack bar or cafeteria. List costs for any of these items that are available. The more information available to participants at this stage, the fewer disappointments there will be on tournament day, and all involved can concentrate their energies on play.

5. Obtain regulation equipment. If regulation equipment and awards are not on hand, this requires immediate attention. You cannot always buy an official game ball on short notice, so save yourself the headache and get it early. Awards also take time to prepare; it is important to acquire them early so if an error is made there is time to make the necessary correction.

6. Obtain and organize minor officials and all other staff. A couple of weeks before the tournament, arrange minor officials and other personnel. Distribute a schedule to the officials along with a list of their respective duties. If any officials need training, this is the time to do it. Advise janitorial staff that enough supplies are on hand; extra personnel might be needed to help clean the site during and after the tournament.

7.   Alert the media. Make sure you inform the media of your event so they can make plans to cover it. This might mean contacting the local newspaper and radio and TV stations or simply notifying a school's photography club; in any case, this should be done early.

8.   Check the scoring system. Sufficient scoring forms need to be on hand. Make sure the score clock functions properly.

9.   Arrange signage. A few days ahead, arrange for signs to be prepared that identify the tournament, tell which teams use which change rooms, and direct participants to the gym, bleachers, cafeteria, first-aid room, and change rooms.

10.   Perform a final spot check. The day before the tournament, perform a final check of the facility, the equipment, and the signs to make sure everything is ready to roll. Come in early on tournament day. In spite of good planning, there are often last-minute items that will need your attention. Make a walk-through of the playing site, checking for anything that might be dangerous to participants and ensuring that nets and lines are officially placed, signs are in place, score sheets and extra pencils are at the scoring table, the score clock is working, and anything else that needs attention gets it.

All the schedules in this book assume that you are using only one draw. However, in some sports, such as badminton and tennis, there will be different divisions—for example, men's singles, women's singles, men's doubles, women's doubles, and mixed doubles. At times there may be additional categories for junior and senior players. Usually these events are held at separate times and often on separate days. For example, singles will be held on the first day, and doubles will be held on the early part of the second day, followed by mixed doubles. This method is usually preferred when players can enter two or more categories. If entries are limited to one event, then the preferred method is to alternate the categories in a balanced way. Alternating the categories, with, for instance, men's singles playing one round, followed by a round of women's singles, and so on, gives greater opportunity for participants to receive adequate rest between matches.

When preparing a schedule, keep in mind the best arrival time for the different entries. If two entries are of nearly equal caliber, but one has a greater distance to travel, then the one closer to the playing site should play the earlier game.

1. As soon as possible, and at least a month before the tournament day, the director should
   - ❏ Obtain permission to use, and book, necessary facilities.
   - ❏ Prepare a schedule of play.
   - ❏ Obtain qualified major and minor officials, plus appropriate medical personnel.
   - ❏ Send information about the tournament to all teams involved. This should include a playing schedule, a list of special things to bring to the tournament such as practice balls, and, where appropriate, information regarding such things as maps of playing facilities, accommodation information, and food information.
   - ❏ Ensure that regulation equipment is available.
   - ❏ Ensure that awards are ready and that perpetual trophies will be on hand.

2. At least two weeks before the tournament, the director should
   - ❏ Advise media of the event.
   - ❏ Ensure that adequate supervision will be ready for security and crowd control.
   - ❏ Ensure that all scoring forms are ready.
   - ❏ Ensure that all officials know their duties.
   - ❏ Draw up any necessary tournament committees.

3. The last few days before the tournament, the director should
   - ❏ Ensure that appropriate signs are made up identifying such places as change rooms to be used for teams and the location of the cafeteria.

4. On the day of the tournament, the director should
   - ❏ Do a final check to make sure everything is in place.
   - ❏ Hold a coaches' meeting prior to the event to advise coaches of any last-minute concerns and to answer any questions.
   - ❏ Ensure that all personnel are doing their jobs.
   - ❏ Convene a committee to resolve any questions or disputes that might arise from the tournament.

5. Immediately following the tournament, the director should
   - ❏ Prepare and send out an appropriate media release concerning the tournament.

6. Within a week of the tournament, the director should
   - ❏ Prepare and send a report to the participating teams and where necessary to senior conveners and executive directors. This report should contain
     a. a summary of the tournament results, including matches, games, and so on and final results,
     b. a report on any meetings held in connection with the tournament,
     c. an expense report, and
     d. recommendations for future tournaments.

Figure 10.1 Tournament checklist.

From *Organizing Successful Tournaments* (3e) by John Byl, 2006, Champaign, IL: Human Kinetics.

Attending to Game Day Duties

Before the first game is to begin you should address three groups of people: the coaches, the athletes, and the spectators. These people are all your guests; remember to treat them that way. Hold a coaches' meeting well before the first game; providing beverages is a thoughtful gesture. Advise coaches of any last-minute concerns and answer any questions they have. Address athletes and spectators early enough to permit a sufficient warm-up for those playing in the first game. Welcome everyone, and summarize key tournament rules, safety considerations, and any other appropriate points. After giving some brief words of encouragement, you are ready to begin the tournament.

Wouldn't it be pleasant if on tournament day you could just sit back and enjoy the day? That is a luxury you won't be free to experience. Your advance planning will certainly make a difference in how hectic things are, but at the least it is your job to make sure your guests are well attended to and all things run as smoothly and as timely as possible. This means monitoring the facility, the officials, the support personnel, the spectators, the schedule, and the clock. You probably will not be able to take in much of the playing action. Because a lot of supervision is needed on tournament day, it is best to remain clear of as much other work as possible, even scoring the results. Trying to wear two caps, such as the tournament director and a coach, is likely to be unsatisfying; you will undoubtedly shortchange your team and your tournament guests.

You'll want to decide in advance whether to schedule a closing ceremony; some tournaments lend themselves better than others to such an event. Unless it is a key game ending the season or a series, participants usually want to return home as soon as possible. If you do host a closing ceremony, be sure to have all necessary results at your disposal as well as any awards you will be giving. If you want to have a celebrity present the awards, arrange this well in advance. If a guest does address the crowd, you act as the emcee, making sure that people are properly introduced. Keep the ceremony moving quickly, but do permit sufficient time for award winners to enjoy their moments in the spotlight.

As the tournament comes to a close, make sure that teams are safely on their way home, officials have been paid, equipment has been returned to its appropriate places, and the playing site has been left in its original condition. Informally thank participants and officials as they leave. Depending on the association or media you are dealing with, a tournament summary might need to go out that day.

Providing a Tournament Summary

Participants and associations like to get a tournament summary as soon as possible. You can create much of the report and cover letter before the tournament begins. Then, when the tournament is over, you will need only to enter some information and do minor editing before you are ready to distribute the report.

Remember to send an official note of appreciation to the officials and others who helped organize and implement the tournament. The gesture is an appropriate courtesy—and it might help you when you need some of these people for your next tournament.

Assigning Committee Responsibilities

For large tournaments, delegating work to committees is very helpful. The following committees should be sufficient to ensure that work is evenly divided and that all tasks of organizing a successful tournament are properly completed:

Tournament director(s)

Participant publicity and services

Officials and playing equipment

Spectator publicity, services, and control

Awards

Finance

• **Tournament director(s).** The tournament director is responsible for overseeing the entire tournament. This person (or committee) bids for the tournament, prepares the draw, and constantly supervises all aspects of the tournament to ensure that it is successfully organized and implemented.

The other committees must complete their work and report to the tournament director any decisions they have made as well as progress they are making on fulfilling their responsibilities. In the early stages, each committee ought to prepare a budget and submit it to the finance committee. When the tournament is completed, each committee should submit a final report, including a summary of the committee's work and recommendations for future tournaments, to the tournament director.

• **Participant publicity and service committee.** This committee is responsible for publicizing the tournament, inviting entries to register, registering the entries, and providing entries with the necessary pretournament and tournament-day services. Pretournament services include providing directions to the playing site and information regarding accommodations and food. Some large tournaments might involve the additional work of providing accommodations. Tournament-day services include such things as on-site refreshments, medical services, game-time amenities, and informational signs. If a tournament banquet is to be provided, this committee should prepare and host it.

• **Officials and playing equipment committee.** This committee's first task is to acquire the services of appropriately certified officials; in the case of minor officials this committee might need to hold several training sessions so these officials do their jobs correctly. This committee's second task is to ensure that regulation equipment is on hand and that the playing area is properly in place, with fields lined, benches in place, and so on. This committee should also acquire and place score sheets, clocks, and other necessary officiating equipment.

• **Spectator publicity, services, and control committee.** This committee is primarily concerned with the spectators. Spectators include those who come to watch any part of the tournament as well as anyone who is interested in hearing about it later. This committee should arrange for adequate seating and refreshment concessions for those who watch. This committee should also administer security to ensure the safety and enjoyment of the spectators and athletes as well as the protection of the playing facility.

- **Awards committee.** This committee is responsible for acquiring appropriate awards. They should also organize the presentation of these awards, which involves deciding who will determine the award winners, who will present the awards, and when awards should be presented.

- **Finance committee.** This committee prepares an overall budget for the tournament and controls the funds throughout the tournament. They are responsible for collecting gate receipts and for paying all the bills.

Staging a Safe Tournament

The safety of participants is vital to staging successful tournaments. The law asks you to plan and implement your tournament as well as any reasonable and prudent tournament director would. Proper planning, adequate and competent supervision, a safe playing site, and written records are instrumental to ensuring a safe tournament for all and protecting yourself from litigation.

Obviously the playing site(s) needs to be safe for all concerned. If a field will be played on, carefully walk the field, looking for any potholes, protruding objects, or rocks that need to be removed before play begins. Perform this check several days in advance and again on tournament day. A written record of both walks should include when you completed the walk, how you did it, and any findings and actions taken. If fields are to be lined, use field-marking chalk or talc powder; avoid lime because it can burn if it contacts the eyes or an open wound.

Follow the same procedures at any indoor sites. It is also wise to prepare a thorough checklist to file with any recommendations for action and a record of follow-up. Just before the tournament, use the list again, with special attention to the areas required for the tournament. Figure 10.2 provides an example of such a form for volleyball.

Date of check _____ Time of check _____ Name of checker _____

Playing site	Okay	attention	Remarks
All lights are working.	_____	_____	_____
All lights are covered with protective screens.	_____	_____	_____
Portable equipment is at least 20 feet from the court.	_____	_____	_____
Protruding hazards are adequately padded.	_____	_____	_____
Spectator and off-court player movement will not interfere with play.	_____	_____	_____

Volleyball concerns			
Net is in good repair.	_____	_____	_____
Net is at regulation height.	_____	_____	_____
Ball is inflated to regulation pressure.	_____	_____	_____
Support posts are adequately padded.	_____	_____	_____
Score table is a safe distance from the court.	_____	_____	_____
Team benches are a safe distance from the court.	_____	_____	_____
Towels are available to wipe spills from refreshment containers.	_____	_____	_____

Figure 10.2 Sample safe-site checklist for volleyball.
From *Organizing Successful Tournaments* (3e) by John Byl, 2006, Champaign, IL: Human Kinetics.

To further decrease the likelihood of injury, use equipment that is up to standard. Adhere to official rules in preparing the playing site. Standard equipment (such as padding for volleyball posts) is imperative. Rule books for most sports state how far the team bench needs to be from the sideline or how much room is needed from the edge of the court to the wall. If the wall is too close, install proper padding to the floor—players must not be able to strike the wall when running or sliding into it. Any objects protruding from the wall that might endanger athletes must be padded. At the beginning of the tournament, advise participants of potential dangers and the precautions you have taken to minimize injuries.

Spectator safety is important as well. Seating should be structurally safe and provide adequate protection from balls or pucks, especially if a sport is new to the community. You might want to cordon off particular areas (for example, to avoid spectator and athlete contact) and advise people to remain in their designated spaces. Depending on the likely emotional intensity of the contest, you might need to arrange for appropriate security. You might feel you should rope off some exits for crowd control, but exercise considerable caution if you do so. In the case of a fire, blocked exits can be deadly.

Verify that the institution sponsoring the tournament is adequately insured. Insurance should cover you and all participants (including officials, players, spectators, and support personnel) at any location being used for the tournament. It might be wise to distribute accountability for the safety of all participants by having participants, or a legal representative of a participating team, sign a waiver form along with the entry. Figures 10.3 and 10.4 are samples of such forms. This form does not, however, protect you against negligent behavior. You should be aware that a parent or guardian cannot sign away the rights of a child; a child could be represented by a lawyer who would file suit in the child's name.

Name _____

Address _____

City _____ State _____ Zip _____

Telephone: Home _____ Business _____

Male _____ Female _____ Birth date _____

T-shirt size: Adult   or   child

Sm _____   Med _____   Lg _____   XL _____

Release form

In consideration of your accepting this entry, I hereby waive all claims against the [sponsor], associated sponsors, and any of their personnel for any injury I might suffer in this event. I hereby attest that I am physically fit and sufficiently prepared for completing the event. Further, I hereby grant full permission for sponsors and organizers to include pictures of me and quotations from me in any legitimate accounts of the [event] and in promotion thereof. If [event] is canceled, my registration fee will be refunded.

Signature _____ Date _____

Figure 10.3   Individual entry form.
From *Organizing Successful Tournaments* (3e) by John Byl, 2006, Champaign, IL: Human Kinetics.

We are honored to host the [tournament name], to be held [date] at [site location]. We would like to see your team participate. The fee for the tournament is [$], payable to [name of institution]. If you are interested, please indicate your intent below and return this form and your payment by [date] to

[Registrar or tournament director's name]

[Complete address]

We will be using certified officials and will ensure that the facility is safe to play in. [An/No] athletic trainer will be on hand. As a legal representative of your team, you realize the inherent dangers in this sport and accept responsibility for the conduct of your team. Should one of your players receive an injury, your institution's insurance policy should adequately cover costs incurred.

Team name _____

Coach's name _____

Coach's phone number _____

Team representative _____

Team representative's signature _____

Team representative's position _____

Team representative's year of birth _____

Date signed _____

Figure 10.4   Invitational tournament form.
From *Organizing Successful Tournaments* (3e) by John Byl, 2006, Champaign, IL: Human Kinetics.

First-aid procedures, supplies, and personnel need to be in place and accessible on tournament day. It has been suggested that anyone who coaches should be able to administer first aid, including cardiopulmonary resuscitation, and maintain current certification. The same could be said for you as tournament director. Procedures for dealing with injuries must be clearly defined in writing and understood by all concerned. These procedures should include such details as responsibilities of personnel, the location of the nearest telephone, emergency numbers, the extent and nature of treatment permitted, and the necessity for filing a follow-up report. Once again, documentation is important. You can use the National Safety Council's Standard Student Activity Form when recording this information.

Screening entries is a factor in tournament safety; players or teams with a large disparity in skill levels should not face each other. I have observed a novice badminton player lose eyesight in one eye after playing a tournament game against an experienced opponent. Had this mismatch not occurred, the injury would have been less likely. Either limit your entrants to those of similar caliber or choose a tournament type that will quickly separate novices from experienced players. This is safer for participants and also makes for more meaningful play.

Finally, when tournament day arrives, highlight for participants the important components of your safety plan, noting fire exits, any potential hazards on the playing site, and what to do in case of an injury. If an athletic therapist is available, advise injured participants not to move until he or she arrives.

Concerns over litigation are real and justified, but they should not scare you away from taking on the responsibilities of organizing a tournament. If you act reasonably and with prudence, you are not likely to need to defend yourself against a charge of negligence. More important, the participants in your tournament will have enjoyed safe play. For a more detailed understanding of sport law, read *Coaches' Guide of Sport Law* by Gary Nygaard and Thomas Boone (Champaign, IL: Human Kinetics, 1985).

ABOUT THE AUTHOR

© John Byl

John Byl, PhD, is a professor of physical education at Redeemer University College in Ancaster, Ontario, Canada, where he teaches courses including Organization of Sport and Physical Education. He has directed high school and college intramurals for more than 30 years and has coached a variety of sports at the community, high school, and college levels. He also has served as an advisor on league and tournament formats, preparing the schedule for the Women United Soccer Association (WUSA) in its last year of competition.

Byl has authored and coauthored several books, including 101 Fun Warm-Up and Cool-Down Games, Intramural Recreation: Step-by-Step Guide to Creating an Effective Program, and Co-Ed Recreational Games. He served as the president of the Canadian Intramural Recreation Association (CIRA) of Ontario and vice president of SportHamilton and the Ontario Colleges Athletic Association. Byl earned his PhD in organization, administration and policy from SUNY-New York, a master's degree in human kinetics from the University of Windsor, and a bachelor's degree in physical education from the University of British Columbia.

HOW TO USE THIS CD

Organizing Successful Tournaments, Third Edition CD-ROM

This CD-ROM contains over 1,000 schedule templates that users can download to create various tournaments based on their individual needs. Created exclusively for coaches, athletic directors, and PE teachers, you will find information on creating schedules, brackets, seeds, and byes for round robin, single- and double-elimination, league, multilevel tournaments, and extended tournaments. By following the directions below and referring to the text you will be able to create a perfectly tailored tournament quickly and efficiently.

Minimum System Requirements

You can use this CD-ROM on either a Windows®-based PC or a Macintosh computer.

Windows

- IBM PC compatible with Pentium® processor
- Windows® 98/2000/XP
- Microsoft® Word
- At least 16 MB RAM with 32 MB recommended
- 4x CD-ROM drive
- Inkjet or laser printer (optional)
- 256 colors
- Mouse

Macintosh

- Power Mac® recommended
- System 9.x or higher
- Microsoft® Word for Macintosh
- At least 16 MB RAM with 32 MB recommended
- 4x CD-ROM drive
- Inkjet or laser printer (optional)
- 256 colors
- Mouse

Getting Started

Microsoft® Windows®

1. Select the "My Computer" icon from your desktop.
2. Select the CD-ROM drive.
3. Select the file you want to use from the CD-ROM and double-click to open the file.
4. On the task bar click on "Table," then "Hide Gridlines." If the option says, "Show the Gridlines," leave it alone and go back to the file.
5. Complete the information in the appropriate fields, starting with Competition Name. Use the Tab key to enter the information and proceed to the next text field.
6. When you enter text in the last Time text field, be sure to Tab to enter the data. The schedule is now complete.
7. Save the schedule with your desired file name.
8. Print the schedule on paper or save as a Web page, if desired.

Macintosh

1. Double-click the CD icon located on the desktop.
2. Select the file you want to use from the CD-ROM and double-click to open the file.
3. On the task bar click on "Table," then "Hide Gridlines." If the option says, "Show the Gridlines," leave it alone and go back to the file.
4. Complete the information in the appropriate fields, starting with Competition Name. Use the Tab key to enter the information and proceed to the next text field.
5. When you enter text in the last Time text field, be sure to Tab to enter the data. The schedule is now complete.
6. Save the schedule with your desired file name.
7. Print the schedule on paper or save as a Web page, if desired.

For customer support:

If you need software technical support or, if the schedule you are looking for is not available, please contact John Byl at byl@redeemer.on.ca to discuss customized schedules or technical support problems. PowerPoint programs are available for coaches at http://www.redeemer.n.ca/~byl/schedules/powerpointslides.